The Cour[...]
Stand A[...]

*(Conversations with
U.G. Krishnamurti)*

Transcribed and Edited
ELLEN J. CHRYSTAL

Foreword by
MAHESH BHATT

Smriti Books

ISBN: 81-87967-06-4

First Edition: 2001
Reprint Edition: 2002
Third Edition: 2005

© Design & Presentation: Smriti Books

Publishers
SMRITI BOOKS
(an imprint of)
SPB Enterprises
124, Siddhartha Enclave,
New Delhi-110 014 (INDIA)
Email: smritibooks@vsnl.net
sunita@smritibooks.com
Website: www.spbenterprises.net
Works : B-219 Sector 31
Noida-201303 (U.P.) INDIA

Distributors
NEW AGE BOOKS
A-44 Naraina Phase-I
New Delhi-110 028 (INDIA)
Email: nab@vsnl.in
Website: www.newagebooksindia.com

Printed in India
at Shri Jainendra Press
A-45 Naraina Phase-I, New Delhi-110 028

*My teaching, if that is the word you want to use,
has no copyright. You are free to reproduce,
distribute, interpret, misinterpret, distort, garble,
do what you like, even claim authorship,
without my consent or the permission of anybody.*

U.G.

PUBLISHER'S NOTE

All of U.G.'s books declare that his teachings have no copyright, and that to publish and to distribute them, requires no permission. Yet, we felt that we must somehow get in touch with U.G. and inform him of our desire to publish and distribute his works. Permission may not be needed, but blessings are always required.

We got in touch with Mahesh Bhatt, an eminent filmmaker of India, an ardent disciple of U.G. On learning about our intentions, he not only gave us his encouragement but also wrote a foreword for all the books. So here they are, a tribute to the great mystic from us....

CONTENTS

Publisher's Note   4

Foreword – *Mahesh Bhatt*   7

A Note About U.G. – *Jeffrey Moussaieff Masson*   11

Editor's Note – *Henk Schoenville*   15

PART I

You Don't Have To Do a Thing   17

PART II

I Cannot Create the Hunger in You   49

PART III

Nice Meeting You, and Goodbye   85

Afterword – *Ellen Chrystal*   123

FOREWORD

"What's your message for mankind on this Teacher's Day, U.G.?" I hollered on the overseas phone-call, preparing myself for a very subversive answer from the man from whom I have learnt the most important lessons of my life. A brief silence echoed over the phone-static: it was late night in New York and I had pulled U.G. out of bed. "All teachers should be destroyed!" he pronounced, "It is they who are responsible for the mess you find yourselves in. I'm not a teacher and have never been one, but don't you see what a mess the messiahs have left the world in?" "Yes, U.G." I whispered, "Thank you and goodbye." He laughed as he hung up the phone, knowing very well what a shattering impact what he had just said would have on me.

Here was a man who I had always framed in my mind as the greatest teacher I've ever known dismissing the very awe with which I held him. What was this man, I wondered. After knowing him for twenty years, here I was still struggling to define him.

I remember the time when a friend of mine, in fact the person who had introduced me to U.G., out of frustration from not being able to answer this question, put the query, "What is U.G. Krishnamurthy?" to the Chinese I-Ching. He received the following answer: "He's not a guru, not a priest, not a savant and certainly not a teacher. He has no interest in enlightening you and in fact does not intend to do anything. He burns with passion and without purpose. He's as lost without you as you're without him.

His light dies if you do not reflect it. Your life is dark without his light." And often when your head reels with the roller-coaster ride that U.G. puts you on, and you moan, "Oh God!" he immediately pipes up, "Why bring that guy into it? What has he got to do with anything?"

No God, no teaching, no spiritual salvation, no hope—U.G. offers you none of these. On the contrary, he demolishes every-thing you've ever stood for. Once, when we were driving to the Geneva airport and a full moon was rising in the dark, wintry Swiss sky, he said something I'll never forget. He said, "Unless human-kind comes to terms with the blunt truth that it is no more important than the mosquito or the field rat, it is doomed." This individual called U.G. is just an animal, nothing more. Whatever I say cannot be used to promote myself or promote any cause for the welfare of mankind. What I say undermines the very founda-tion of human thought. How can society be interested in what I say? When this body drops dead it will be recycled by nature just like a garden slug to enrich the soil. In short it will just rot. If you want comfort go to the gurus. They will sell it to you. I don't give a damn for all the teachers that existed before me. They were con-men, they conned themselves, and conned the whole of mankind and we're all going to pay a heavy price for their con-game." Courage! Unheldback, furious, certain courage—that's what distin-guishes U.G. for me and that's what he evokes in me. No one in the history of the world has had the courage to blast authority the way he has and yet no one has stared at one's own insignificance as boldly in the eye.

When I look back at my life with its successes and its failures and its endless errors, I know that had it not been for U.G. I probably would not be in the position where I would be asked to write this foreword today. And yet he fiercely rejects taking any credit for whatever I achieved in my life. Once while sitting in a coffee shop I asked him, "Is there nothing you want from me U.G.?" He replied, "Only one thing. After I'm dead and gone there should be no trace of me inside of you and outside of you." This complete self-smashing jolted my entire being. His will to stand alone and then just die quietly washed me head to toe. I've always without question and with absolute consent done everything he has asked me to do, but I wonder if I'll ever be able to fulfill this impossible "wish" he has wished for me. Because I know for certain that the day U.G. fades out from my heart, that'll be the end of me and all I know.

Mahesh Bhatt
Mumbai, India
October 2000

A Note about U.G.

Jeffrey Moussaieff Masson

*N*eti neti was the way the old Upsanishads characterized wisdom: Not this, not that. You could not characterize it. So it is with U.G. Krishnamurti. Try having a dialogue with somebody about him, and watch the trouble you get into.

Friend: I heard you went to visit U.G. Krishnamurti last night. I don't really know who he is. Can you tell me?

Me: (The minute I try to tell people about him, I realize I am doing a terrible job of describing him.) He is an anti-guru guru. Well, not really. A man totally opposed to teaching.

Friend: What does he do?

Me: Well, he teaches. No, that's not it. He sits around in other people's homes.

Friend: So he lives off other people?

Me: No. He is independently wealthy. Well, not wealthy. Just independent.

Friend: And what does he sit around doing?

Me: Talking. About gurus, and how much he hates them, and what phonies they all are, every one of them.

Friend: Who listens to him?

Me: A group of people. I know what you are thinking, but no, they are not disciples at all. They are anti-disciples.

Friend: How does that show?

Me: Well, they make fun of him, they argue with him, they insult him. They do anything but treat him as a guru. And if they do (and some attempt it) he becomes abusive, angry, contemptuous. He genuinely does not like it.

Friend: But he seems to have something of the same format as the guru: he travels to countries where people hear about him and they come to listen to him speak. He speaks. He preaches, or rather he anti-preaches.

Me: You are right. Everything he does is the mirror-image of what the guru does, in reverse. He turns everything upside down. This is the part of the attraction for people. He is fascinating to watch. I have seen my own father, a guru seeker for the last 60 years, sit mesmerized in front of him, resisting with all his strength U.G.'s resistance against making him a guru. My father wants him to be a guru, longs for him to be a guru, but paradoxically winds up admiring him *à la folie* precisely for *not* being a guru. So much so, though, that U.G. is his guru.

The same is true, I feel for others, such as Julie, the marvelous Julie. She runs to him. He smacks her (figuratively speaking; that is, he insults her). Julie flies to Bangalore to be with him. "Get away from here," he tells her, "your worship nauseates me." He means it. She looks for the zen koan in his comment. He wants her to stop, but she insists he is teaching her via parable, paradox — instruction by insult. Yet, he is also found of her, he can't help himself, everybody is. She won't let go. She is wealthy and offers him a house, an apartment, an income. He scorns her. He is genuinely disgusted, angry. He doesn't need it, and if he did he wouldn't take it. Yet she keeps coming back. And he keeps letting her back.

The same dance with a hundred different steps with other "friends" (the only term he will accept). He is compelling, no question of it.

And me? Where do I stand in all of this? I like him, as who would not. He is fun, he is entirely human, he is deliciously unspiritual. He is smart and quick and affectionate. A friend. But why, when I go to see this friend, do I find myself talking so much about gurus, and anti-gurus, and the whole phenomenon? Why is *he* so interested in this topic too? He repeats himself. I repeat myself. He comes to California, I go to visit him. We both talk about how many phonies there are in the world of gurus. Is this a subtle way of saying that he is not one of those phonies? No, it is a genuine comment, an observation. But he makes it in a thousand different ways, over and over, *ad nauseum*. And yet, it is never boring. It is infinitely fascinating.

The main reason for this fascination is the person in front of me, U.G. Krishnamurti himself. For while he abjures every single attribute of the guru, he also speaks of a strange life. Bizarre things have happened to him that have not happened to other ordinary people (but are strangely parallel to mystic experiences in reverse).

He had a "calamity" that nearly killed him physically. He speaks of it obscurely. Other mystics are "illuminated." He is anti-illuminated, powerfully. Everything he is is calculated to be as unlike the traditional guru as possible. And yet, even if for the opposite reason, he, too, has no desires, he does not sleep, he does not dream, he eats no meat. There is some compelling purity about him, some way in which he captures a kind of longing that we all seem to have for a genuinely wise human being.

I would not be afraid to characterize U.G. as a man of wisdom, not quite like the one described in the *Bhagavadgita* (the Sthitaprajna) but not entirely unlike him either. A paradox, a wonder, a marvel, a fine human being.

Jeffrey Moussaieff Masson
Berkeley, California
November 1995

Jeffrey Masson is the author of *Final Analysis: The Making and Unmaking of a Psychoanalyst; Against Therapy; The Oceanic Feeling: The Origins of Religious Sentiment in Ancient India; My Father's Guru: A Journey through Spirituality and Disillusion; When Elephants Weep.*

EDITOR'S NOTE

Henk Schoenville

In July 1978, U.G. invited me to come to Bangalore, where he was staying and from where he arranged his travels in those times. My immediate answer was, "Yes Sir, I would like to." At the same time I reminded him of my invitation to him a year before to come to Amsterdam: "Many people are there waiting to see you, Sir." U.G. finally came to Amsterdam in 1982, and stayed (much to his own surprise) for 21 days in a beautiful house offered by some friends.

U.G. fell in love — as most foreign visitors do — with Amsterdam and its beautiful canals and flowers. The city must have affected him, as could be seen in his clear and powerful talks. Many visitors came to see and talk to him. Among them were psychologists, publishers, spiritual journalists, and sannyasins, hashish-smoking "freaks" and "flower" people. One of them was a well-known poet who had just won an award for "talking without a break for 24 hours." (U.G. silenced him with one sentence!) So, they were quite a mixed bag — still, I would say they were "ordinary" people.

Fortunately, we had installed a tape recorder, and with U.G.'s permission, almost all of his talks (some 24 hours of material) were recorded. After U.G.'s visit was over, it occurred to me that I could easily produce an audiotape out of that material, primarily for the use of friends. The effort ended up in the series of three cassettes entitled, "Give Up."

I first edited the tapes around September and October of 1982. Since then many copies of "Give Up" have found their way around the globe. People have called me from Germany, France, Austria, Australia, Italy, the United States — altogether from more than 14 countries. Every year since then, whenever we met, U.G. has remarked, "It seems you have done something tremendous. Everyone is praising your tapes, wherever I go." In this printed version we have changed the title of these talks to "The Courage to Stand Alone."

U.G. once said to his visitors, while sitting outside his chalet in Gstaad, Switzerland, "It is nice of you to come here, but you have come to the wrong place — because you want an answer, and you think that my answer will be your answer. But that is not so. I may have found my answer, but that is not your answer. You have to find out for yourself and by yourself the way in which you are functioning in this world, and that will be your answer." I hope these words of U.G.'s will help you to find "the courage to stand on your own solid feet."

Henk Schoenville
Amsterdam, Holland
July, 1995

16

Part I

YOU DON'T HAVE TO DO A THING

Q : U.G., do you agree with me that you live in a frictionless state?

U.G.: Not in conflict with the society. This is the only reality I have, the world as it is today. The ultimate reality that man has invented has absolutely no relationship whatsoever with the reality of this world. As long as you are seeking, searching, and wanting to understand that reality (which you call "ultimate reality," or call it by whatever name you like), it will not be possible for you to come to terms with the reality of the world exactly the way it is. So, anything you do to escape from the reality of this world will make it difficult for you to live in harmony with the things around you.

We have an idea of harmony. How to live at peace with yourself — that's an idea. There is an extraordinary peace that is there already. What makes it difficult for you to live at peace with yourself is the creation [of the idea] of what you call "peace," which is totally unrelated to the harmonious functioning of this body. When you free yourself from the burden of reaching out there to grasp, to experience, and to be in that reality, then you will find that you have no way of experiencing the reality of anything, but at least you will not be living in a world of illusions. You will accept that there is nothing, nothing that you can do to experience the reality of anything, except the reality that is imposed on us by society. We have to accept the reality as it is imposed on us by society because it is very essential for us to function in this world intelligently and sanely. If we don't accept that reality, we are lost. We will end up in the loony bin. So we have to accept the reality as it is imposed on us by the culture, by society or whatever you want to call it, and at the same time understand that there is nothing that we can do to experience the reality of anything. Then you will not be in conflict with the society, and the demand to be something other than what you are also will come to an end.

The goal that you have placed before yourself, the goal which you have accepted as the ideal goal to be reached, and the demand to be something other than what you are, are no longer there. It is not a question of accepting anything, but the pursuit of those goals which the culture has placed before us, and which we have accepted as desirable, is not there any more. The demand to reach that goal also is not there any more. So, you are what you are.

When the movement in the direction of becoming something other than what you are isn't there any more, you are not in conflict with yourself. If you are not in conflict with yourself, you cannot be in conflict with the society around you. As long as you are not at peace with yourself, it is not possible for you to be at peace with others. Even then there is no guarantee that your neighbors will be peaceful. But, you see, you will not be concerned with that. When you are at peace with yourself, then you are a threat to society as it functions today. You will be a threat to your neighbors because they have accepted the reality of the world as real, and they are also pursuing some funny thing called "peace." You will become a threat to their existence as they know it and as they experience it. So you are all alone — not the aloneness that people want to avoid — you are all alone.

It is not ultimate reality that one is really interested in, not the teachings of the gurus, not the teachings of the holy men, not the umpteen number of techniques you have, which will give you the energy which you are seeking. Once that movement [of thought] is not there, that will set in motion and release the energy that is there. It doesn't have to be the holyman's teaching. It doesn't have to be any techniques that man has invented — because there is no friction there. You really don't know what it is.

The movement there [*pointing to the listeners*] and the movement here [*pointing to himself*] is one and the same. The human machine is no different from the machine out there. Both of them are in unison. Whatever energy is there, the same energy is in operation here. So, any energy you experience through the practice of any techniques is a frictional energy. That energy is created by the friction of thought — the demand to experience that energy is responsible for the energy you experience. But this energy is something which cannot be experienced at all. This is just an expression of life, a manifestation of life. You don't have to do a thing.

Anything you do to experience that [energy] is preventing the energy which is already there, which is the expression of life, which is the manifestation of life, from functioning. It has no value in terms of the values we give to whatever we are doing — the techniques, meditation, yoga and all that. I am not against any one of those things. Please don't get me wrong. But they are not the means to achieve the goal that you have placed before yourself — the goal itself is false. If the suppleness of the body is the goal you have before you, probably the techniques of yoga will help you to keep the body supple. But that is not the instrument to reach the goal of enlightenment or transformation or whatever you want to call it. Even the techniques of meditation are self-centered activities. They are all self-perpetuating mechanisms which you use. So the object of your search for the ultimate reality is defeated by all these techniques because these techniques are self-perpetuating instruments. You will suddenly realize, or it will dawn on you, that the very search for the ultimate reality is also a self-perpetuating mechanism. There is nothing to reach, nothing to gain, nothing to attain.

As long as you are doing something to attain your goal, it is a self-perpetuating mechanism. I use the words "self-perpetuating mechanism," but I don't mean that there is a self or an entity. I have to use the word "self" because there is no other word. It's like the self-starter you have in the car. It perpetuates itself. That is all that it is interested in. Anything you want to achieve is a self-centered activity. When I use the term "self-centered activity," you always translate it in terms of something that should be avoided, because selflessness is your goal. As long as you are doing something to be selfless, you will be a self-centered individual. When this movement in the direction of wanting to be a selfless man is not there, then there is no self and there is no self-centered activity. So it is the very techniques, the systems and methods which you are using to reach your goal of selflessness, which are self-centered activities.

Unfortunately, society has placed that goal [selflessness] before us as the ideal goal, because a selfless man will be a great asset to the society and society is interested only in continuity — the status quo. So all those values, which we have accepted as values that one should cultivate, are invented by the human mind to keep itself going.

The goal is what is making it possible for you to continue in this way, but you are not getting anywhere. The hope is that one day, through some miracle or through the help of somebody, you will be able to reach the goal. It is the hope that keeps you going, but actually and factually you are not getting anywhere. You will realize somewhere along the line that whatever you are doing to reach your goal is not leading you anywhere. Then you will want to try this, that, and the other. But if you try one and you see that it doesn't work, you will see that all the other systems are exactly the same. This has to be very, very clear, you see.

Whatever pursuit you are indulging in, somewhere along the line it has to dawn on you that it is not leading you anywhere. As long as you want something, you will do that. That want has to be very, very clear. What do you want? All the time, I ask you the question, "What do you want?" You say, "I want to be at peace with myself." That is an impossible goal for you to reach because everything you are doing to be at peace with yourself is what destroying the peace that is already there. You have set in motion the movement of thought which is destroying the peace that is there, you see. It is very difficult to understand that all that you are doing is the one thing that is disturbing the harmony, the peace that is already there. Any movement [of thought], in any direction, on any level, is a very destructive factor for the smooth and peaceful functioning of this living organism which is not at all interested in your spiritual experiences. It has no interest in any one of those spiritual experiences, however extraordinary they may be.

When once you have one spiritual experience there is bound to be a demand for more and more of the same, and ultimately you will want to be in that state permanently. There is no such thing as permanent happiness or permanent bliss at all. You think that there is, because all those books talk of eternal bliss, permanent bliss, or permanent happiness. Yet you know jolly well that it [the pursuit] is not leading you anywhere. So, the mechanism that is involved, the instrument that you are using, is the one thing that keeps you going because it does not know anything else. It has come into being through so many years of hard work, effort and will. Your wanting to be in a state of effortlessness through the use of effort is not going to succeed. So forget about the effortless state — it doesn't exist at all. You want to achieve an effortless state through effort — how the hell are you going to achieve that goal? You forget that everything that you are doing, any movement that is there, any want that is there, for whatever reason, *is* effort.

Effortlessness is something which cannot be achieved through effort. Anything that you do to stop the effort, is itself an effort. It's really a maddening thing! You have not really pushed yourself into that corner. If you do, then you will really go crazy; but you are frightened of that. You have to see that everything that you are doing to be in that effortless state, for whatever reason you want to be there, is effort. Even wanting not to use effort also is effort. The total absence of will and the total absence of effort, all and every kind, may be called an effortless state — but that effortless state is not something that you can achieve through effort.

If you could understand the meaninglessness of what you are doing — you can change the techniques, you can change the teachers, but basically and essentially, the very teaching that you are using to reach your goal is the obstacle. It doesn't matter what teacher you follow. If you question the teaching, unfortunately, you have to question the teacher himself — but then comes the sentiment: "Something is wrong with me, one day I am going to understand." If it is not possible for you to understand today, you are not going to understand at all. So the understanding is the absence of the demand for understanding — now or tomorrow.

Now there is no understanding necessary. The understanding is only for the purpose of understanding something tomorrow — not today. Today you don't have to understand a thing at all.

It may sound funny to you, but that's the way it is. So what do you want to understand? You can't understand me at all. I have been talking for 20 days and I can go on, but you are not going to understand anything at all. It's not that it is difficult. It is so simple. The complex structure that is involved is the very thing that does not accept the simplicity of it. That is really the problem. "It can't be that simple," you think, because that structure is so complex that it doesn't want even to consider the possibility that it could be so simple. So you are going to understand tomorrow, not today. Tomorrow it is the same story and then after 10 years it is the same story. So what do you do about this situation? We all have been through that. Either you flip or fly. The chances of flipping are really good if you push yourself into a corner. You are not going to do that.

What do you want to understand? I am not saying anything profound. I have been repeating the same thing day after day, day after day. Basically, it sounds very contradictory to you. What I am doing — you don't understand what I am doing — I make a statement, and the second statement negates the first statement. Sometimes you see contradictions in what I am saying. Actually they are not contradictions. This statement does not express what I am trying to express, so the second statement is negating the first statement; and the third statement is negating the first two statements; the fourth statement is negating the previous three statements. Not with the idea of arriving at any goal. Not with the idea of communicating anything to you. There is nothing to be communicated. Only this series of negations. Not with the idea of arriving at any goal. Your goal is understanding. You want to understand, you see. There is nothing to understand here. Every time you make some sense out of it, I try to point out that is not it. It is not the doctrine of neti-neti.

You know, in India they have evolved this negative approach. But the so-called negative approach is a positive approach, because they are still interested in reaching a goal. They have failed through the positive approaches, so they have invented what is called the negative approach. "Not this, not this, not this." The unknown cannot be reached, you see, nor can it be experienced through the positive approach. The so-called negative approach is not really a negative approach because there is still the positive goal of knowing the unknown, or wanting to experience something — which cannot be experienced. It's only a trick. That's all it is — playing with itself. As long as the goal is a positive goal, no matter what the goal is — whether it is called positive or negative — it is not a negative approach, it is a positive approach.

It's all right to play games, it's interesting, but there is no such thing as "the beyond," no such thing as "the unknown." If you accept that there is such a thing as the unknown, you will do something or the other to know the unknown. Your interest is to know.

So this movement is not going to stop as long as it is interested in experiencing something that cannot be experienced. There is no such thing as the unknown at all. How can I say that there is no such thing as the unknown? How can I make such a dogmatic assertion — you will find out. As long as you are pursuing the unknown, this movement is in operation. There is something that you can do — that gives you the hope that maybe one day you will stumble into this experience of the unknown. How can the unknown ever become the known. Not a chance. Even assuming for a moment that this movement (which is demanding to know the unknown) is not there, what is there you will never know. You have no way of knowing it at all, no way of capturing that and experiencing that or giving expression to it.

So to talk of that bliss, the eternal bliss, love — all of that is romantic poetry. Because you have no way of capturing that and containing it and giving expression to it. So it may dawn on you that this is not the instrument that can help you to understand anything, and there is no other instrument. Then there is nothing to understand.

I don't want to give a talk. You help me.

You see, if you translate what I am saying in terms of your values, in terms of particular codes of conduct, you are really missing the point. It is not that I am against the moral codes of conduct. They have a social value. They are essential for the smooth functioning of society. You have to have some code of conduct to function in this world intelligently. Otherwise there will be utter chaos in this world. That is a social problem. It is not an ethical problem, nor a religious problem. You see, you have to separate the two things because we are living in a different world today. We have to find another way of keeping ourselves in harmony with the world around us. As long as you are in conflict within yourself, it will not be possible for you to be in harmony with the society around you. You are yourself responsible for that.

I am afraid if you translate the statements that I am making within the framework of your religious thinking, you are really missing the point. It has nothing to do with religion at all. I am not suggesting that you should change yourself into something other than what you are. It is just not possible. I am not trying to free you from anything. I don't think there is any purpose in this talking. You can brush aside my description and say it is nonsense, that's your privilege. But maybe it will occur to you that the image you have of your goal, or image of what you are going to do one day through all the effort and will which you are using, has absolutely no relationship whatsoever with what I am describing. What I am describing is not really what you are interested in.

I was telling you the other day, I wish I could give you just a glimpse of it. Not glimpse in the sense in which you use the word "glimpse." A touch of it. You wouldn't want to touch this at all. And what you want, what you are interested in, doesn't exist. You can have a lot of petty experiences, if that is what you are interested in. Do all the meditations, do everything you want, you will have lots of them [experiences]. It's a lot easier to experience those things by taking drugs. I am not recommending drugs, but they are the same, exactly the same. The doctors say that drugs will damage the brain, but meditation will also damage the brain if it is done very seriously. They have gone crazy, jumped into the river and killed themselves. They did all kinds of things — locked themselves up in caves — because they couldn't face it.

You see, it is not possible for you to watch your thoughts, it is not possible for you to watch every step you take. It will drive you crazy. You can't walk. That's not what is meant by this idea that you should be aware of everything — watch every thought — how is it possible for you to watch every thought of yours — and for what do you want to watch your thoughts? What for? Control? It's not possible for you to control. It is a tremendous momentum.

When you succeed in your imagination, that you have controlled your thoughts and experienced some space between those thoughts or some state of thoughtlessness, you feel that you are getting somewhere. That is a thought-induced state of thoughtlessness, a space between two thoughts. The fact that you experience the space between two thoughts and the thoughtless state means that the thought was very, very much there. It surfaces afterwards like the river Rhone which flows through France, disappears and then comes up again. It has gone underground. The river is still there. You can't use it for purposes of navigation, but ultimately it comes up again. In exactly the same way, all these things which you are pushing down into the subterranean regions (feeling that you are experiencing something extraordinary), surface again — and then you will find that those thoughts are welling up inside of you.

You are not aware that you are breathing now. You don't have to be conscious of your breathing. Why do you want to be conscious of your breathing? To control your breathing, to expand your lungs, to do what you like with your chest — that's a different matter. But why do you want to be aware of the movement of breath from the origin to the end? You suddenly become conscious of your breathing. Your breath and thought are very closely related.

That's why you want to control your breath. And that, in a way, is controlling your thought for a while. But if you hold your breath for long, it is going to choke you to death in exactly the same way anything you do to hold or block the flow of thoughts is going to choke you to death, literally to death, or damage something. Thought is a very powerful vibration, an extraordinary vibration. It is like an atom. You can't play with those things.

You are not going to reach your goal of completely controlling your thought. Thought has to function in its own way, in its disconnected, disjointed way. That is something which cannot be brought about through any effort of yours. It has to fall into its normal rhythm. Even if you want to make it fall into a normal rhythm, you are adding momentum to that. It has a life of its own which has, unfortunately, established a parallel life within the movement of life. These two are always in conflict. That will come to an end only when the body comes to an end.

Thought has become the master of this body. Thought has totally mastered the whole thing. It is still trying to control everything that is there. You cannot pull the servant out of the household, no matter what you do. If you forcibly do it, he will burn the whole household, even knowing very well that he will also be burned. It's a foolish thing for him, but that's what you are going to do if you try. Don't push these similes to the logical conclusion, but find out for yourself when you do these things, not just take them lightly. Or, take them lightly and play with them, it's all right. Toys.

Q: Just float along? Nothing to pursue, just float?

U.G.: Even that "floating" is not a voluntary thing on your part. You don't have to do a thing. You are not separate from that.

That's all that I am emphasizing. You cannot separate yourself from the thought and say "these are my thoughts." That is the illusion you have, and you cannot be without any illusion. You always replace one illusion with another illusion. Always!

Q: And I accept that as well.

U.G.: You accept that you are always replacing one illusion with another illusion; so your wanting to be free from illusion is an impossibility. That itself is an illusion. Why do you want to be free from illusions? That's the end of you. It's not that I am frightening you, I am just pointing out that it is not just a lighthearted game to play. That is you, you as you know yourself. When that knowledge you have of yourself is not there any more, the knowledge you have about the world also is not, and cannot be, there any more. It is not going to come to an end that easily. It will always be replaced by another illusion.

You don't want to be a normal person, you don't want to be an ordinary person. That is really the problem. It is the most difficult thing to be an ordinary person. Culture demands you must be something other than what you are. That has created a certain momentum — a tremendous, powerful movement of thought which demands that you should be something other than what you are. That's all that it is. You can use it to achieve something, otherwise it has no use.

The only use you have for thought is to feed this body, and to reproduce. That's all the use you have for thought. It has no other use at all. It cannot be used to speculate.

You can build a tremendous philosophical structure of

thought, but it has no value at all. You can interpret any event in your life, and build up another philosophical structure of thought, but it [thought] is not intended for that.

At the same time, you forget that everything you have around you is the creation of thought. You are yourself born out of thought, otherwise you would not be here at all. In that sense it has a tremendous value, yet it is the very thing that will destroy you.

That's the paradox. Everything that you have created in this world has become possible through the help of that thought, but unfortunately that very thing has become the enemy of man, because you are using thought for purposes for which it is not intended. It can be used for solving the technical problems very well and efficiently, but it cannot be used to solve the problems of life.

Positive thinking, positive living, very interesting, you know. You can't always be positive. How can you be positive? Anything that does not suggest your positive thinking, you call it negative. But positive and negative are only in the field of your thinking. When the thought is not there, it [what is there] is neither positive nor negative. As I was saying, there is no such thing as a negative approach at all. It's a gimmick.

I am telling you to stand on your own — you can walk, you can swim, you are not going to sink. That's all that I can say. As long as there is fear, the danger of your sinking is almost certain. Otherwise, there is a buoyancy there in the water that keeps you afloat. The fear of sinking is the very thing that makes it impossible for you to let the movement happen in its own way. You see, it has no direction. It is just a movement with no direction. You are trying to manipulate and channel that movement along a particular direction so that you can have some benefits. You are just a movement without a direction.

Q: Actually as human beings, we are rather fond of thinking. But why is this rather funny animal thinking all the time?

U.G.: I will ask you the question. You tell me, when do you think? Not why do you think. That's not the question. When do you think? I am asking you a question, when do you think?

Q: As far as I know, all the time.

U.G.: All the time, and for what? What is responsible for your thinking? When do you think? When you want something, that's when you think. It is very clear to me.

Q: Not at all.

U.G.: Of course. You don't even know that you are thinking. Do you know that you are thinking now? It's an automatic thing.

Q: It's an automatic thing, that's right.

U.G.: You don't even know that you are thinking and so why this sudden interest in wanting to find out why you are thinking? I don't even know that I am talking. You don't even know that you are talking. When you asked your questions, "Am I thinking," you would say, "Yes". That "yes" also is an automatic thing.

Q: I don't care if it's automatic.

31

U.G.: The whole thing is on automatic. Whatever is put in there, when you are stimulated, it comes out. In the jargon of computer language, the input has to be there. So, this has been going on and on and on and on. When there is stimulation, it comes out. If it [the stimulation] is not there, you see, it [thinking] stops. So that's the reason why you go on acquiring this knowledge, feeding it all the time.

So, what do you know? You know a lot. You have gathered all this knowledge from various sources and filled it [the mind] up. Most of it is not necessary. You know a lot and you want to know more and more and more — to use it. Of course. There's no such thing as knowledge for the sake of knowledge. It gives you power. Knowledge is power. "I know; you don't know." That gives you power. You may not even be conscious that knowing more than the other gives you power. In that sense, knowledge is power. To acquire more and more knowledge, other than the knowledge that is essential for the survival of the living organism, is to acquire more and more power over others.

The technical knowledge that you need to make a living is understandable. That's all. I have to learn a technique. The society is not going to feed me unless I give something in return. You have to give them what they want, not what you have to give. What have you to give? You have nothing to give anyway. Otherwise what value has this knowledge for you? To know more about something which you really do not know.

We are always talking about thought and thinking. What is thought? Have you ever looked at thought, let alone controlling thought; let alone manipulating thought; let alone using that thought for achieving something material or otherwise. You cannot look at your thought, because you cannot separate yourself from thought and look at it. There is no thought apart from the knowledge you have about those thoughts — the definitions you have. So if somebody asks you the question, "What is thought?" any answer you have is the answer that is put in there — the answers that others have already given.

You have, through combinations and permutations of ideation and mentation about thoughts, created your own thoughts which you call your own. Just as when you mix different colors, you can create thousands of pastel colors, but basically all of them can be reduced to only seven colors that you find in nature. What you think is yours is the combination and permutation of all those thoughts, just the way you have created hundreds and hundreds of pastel colors. You have created your own ideas. That is what you call thinking. When you want to look at thought, what is there is only all you know about thought. Otherwise you can't look at thought. There is no thought other than what is there in what you know about thought. That's all that I am saying. So when that is understood, the meaninglessness of the whole business of wanting to look at thought comes to an end. What is there is only what you know, the definitions given by others. And out of those definitions, if you are very intelligent and clever enough, you create your own definitions. That's all.

When you look at an object, the knowledge you have about that object comes into your head. There is an illusion that thought is something different from objects, but it is you who creates the object. The object may be there, but the knowledge you have about that object is all that you know. Apart from that knowledge, independent of that knowledge, and free from that knowledge, you have no way of knowing anything about it. You have no way of directly experiencing anything. The word "directly" does not mean that there is any other way of experiencing things other than the way you are experiencing things now. The knowledge you have about it is all that is there and that is what you are experiencing. Really, you do not know what it is.

In exactly the same way, when you want to know something about thought, or experience thought, it is the same process that is in operation there. There is no inside or outside. What there is, is only the operation, the flow of the knowledge. So you cannot actually separate yourself from thought and look at it.

So when such a question is thrown at you, what should happen is [the realization] that none of the answers have any meaning, because all that is acquired and taught. So that movement stops. There is no need for you to answer the question. There is no need for you to know anything about it. All that you know comes to a halt. It has no momentum any more. It slows down, and then it dawns upon you that it is meaninglessness to try to answer that question, because it has no answer at all. The answers that others have given are there. So you have nothing to say on that thing called thought, because all you can say is what you have gathered from other sources. You have no answer of your own.

Q: Even then we can have a conversation.

U.G.: All right. All right.

Q: Apart from the question . . .

U.G.: All right, yes.

34

Q: There still are things, like walls and people around you. And what we know about it, what we see about it.

U.G.: But that is not what that person is. You don't actually know anything about that person or that thing, except what you are projecting on that object or the individual. The knowledge you have about it is the experience. It goes on and on. That's all. What that really is, you have no way of knowing.

Q: That is what I understand. When we are speaking about reality, we can only speak of our knowledge about it and call this knowledge reality.

U.G.: What for? Then it becomes a classroom discussion or a discussion in a debating society, each one trying to show that he knows more, a lot more, than the other. What do you get out of it? Each one is trying to prove that he knows more than you, to bring you over to his point of view.

Q: What I am asking is, is there any chance — I understand that there is no method — but is there any chance of getting out of this knowledge of reality to [actual] reality.

U.G.: If you are lucky enough (it's only luck), to get out of this trap of knowledge, the question of reality is not there any more [for you]. The question arises from this knowledge, which is still interested in finding out the reality of things, and to experience directly what that reality is all about. When this [knowledge] is not there, the question is also not there. Then there is no need for finding any answer. This question which you are posing to yourself, and also to me, is born out of the assumption that there is a reality; and that assumption is born out of this knowledge you have of and about the reality. The knowledge is the answer you already have. That is why you are asking the question. The question automatically arises.

What is necessary is not to find out the answer to the question, but to understand that the question which you are asking, posing to yourself, and putting to somebody else, is born out of the answer you already have, which is the knowledge. So, the question and answer format, if we indulge in it for long, becomes a meaningless ritual. If you are really interested in finding reality, what has to dawn on you is that your very questioning mechanism is born out of the answers that you already have. Otherwise there can't be any question.

First of all, there is an assumption on your part that there is a reality, and then, that there is something that you can do to experience that reality. Without the knowledge, [about reality] you have no experience of reality, that is for sure. "If this knowledge is not there, is there any other way of experiencing the reality?" You ask the question. The question goes with the answer. So there is no need to ask questions and there is no need to answer.

I am not trying to be clever. I am just spotlighting what is involved in the question and answer business. I am not actually answering any of your questions. I am just pointing out that you cannot have any questions when you have no answers.

Q: I understand. Even so, I would like to continue the game.

U.G.: Fine. Maybe you are good at the game. I am not. Anyway we will see what we can do.

Q: Even though you know our preoccupation with knowledge, you are talking about reality to us and about accepting reality.

U.G.: As it is.

Q: As it is?

U.G.: As it is imposed on us by our culture for purposes of intelligent and sane functioning in this world, and yet, realizing that it has no value other than its functional value. Because otherwise we will be in trouble, you see. If you don't call this a microphone, and you decide to call it a monkey, we will all have to relearn, and every time we look at it we will have to call it a red or black monkey instead of a microphone. It [thought or language] is very simply for purposes of communication.

Q: I wonder what would happen if we did call that chair a lamp and this table a hat, because a lot of our philosophies and ideas are also linked with it.

U.G.: It is interesting to build a philosophical structure. That's why we have so many philosophers and so many philosophies in this world.

Q: As far as I understand, acceptance is the only thing worth striving for.

U.G.: Don't you see the contradiction in those terms? If you accept, where is the need for striving? It comes to an end. If you accept something, you cannot talk of striving at all. You accept it, you believe. You believe in something, you accept it as an act of faith, and that's the end of it. To question that, means you have not accepted it. You are not sure of it.

Q: I had to accept my job as a legal officer before I could acquire the knowledge that was necessary to get the job.

U.G.: You had to struggle, and put in a lot of effort to acquire the necessary legal knowledge to get the job. That's understood. So, that is the only way. There is no other way. You are applying that same technique to achieve your so-called spiritual goals. This is the difference that I am pointing out. As a legal officer, you know what they do in the courts. You have to rely upon the precedents, and the previous judgments. Both sides quote the previous judgments and argue it out. The judge either accepts your argument or the other fellow's, and he gives a decision either in favor of your client or in favor of your opponent. Then you go to a higher court. There it is the same. Finally you go to the Supreme Court where the judge makes the final decision. You can disagree with the judgment, the client can do everything possible to reject it, and refuse to accept it, but that judgment can be enforced through the law. If it is a civil case you will lose what you are claiming. If it is a criminal matter, you will end up in prison. Ultimately that's the way it is decided who is telling the lie, and who is telling the truth. It is arbitrary in the final analysis.

So it is essential for you to be conversant with the whole structure of the law. It is essential for you to acquire the legal knowledge necessary for your job. The more efficient you are, the better are your chances. The cleverer you are, the better are your prospects. That is understood.

So, you have to put in struggle and effort, use your will and then you arrive at success. There is always more and more to achieve. But you are using that same instrument to achieve your spiritual goals. This is all that I am pointing out.

You cannot conceive of the possibility of understanding anything except in time. Everything takes time. It has taken so many years for you to be where you are today, and you are still striving and struggling to reach a higher plateau — higher and higher and higher. That instrument [mind] which you are using cannot conceive of the possibility of understanding anything without effort, without striving, without producing results. But the issues that you have to deal with in life are the living issues [of how to live]. This [the mind] has not helped us to solve the problems. Temporarily you can find some solution, but that creates another problem, and it goes on and on and on and on. These are all life issues. The living problems. The instrument which we are using [thought] is a dead instrument and cannot be used to understand anything living. You cannot but think in terms of striving, effort, time — one day you are going to reach the spiritual goal — just the way you have succeeded in the goal which you have placed before yourself.

Q: But are you saying that there is some knowledge which solves the real problems of life?

U.G.: No. Not at all. That knowledge cannot help you to understand or solve the living problems. Because there are no problems at all in that sense. We have only the solutions. You are interested only in solutions, and those solutions have not solved your problems. So you are trying to find different kinds of solutions. But the situation will remain exactly the same. There is somehow the hope that maybe you will find *the* solution for solving your problems.

So your problem is not the problem but the solution. If the solution is gone, there is no problem there. If there is a solution, the problem shouldn't be there anymore. If the answers given by others (the "wise men") are the answers, then the questions shouldn't be there at all. So they are obviously not the answers. If they were the answers, the questions would not be there.

Why don't you question the answers? If you question the answers, you must question those who have given the answers. But you take it for granted that they are all wise men; that they are spiritually superior to us all; and that they know what they are talking about. *They don't know a damn thing!*

Why are you asking these questions? — if I may ask you that counter-question. Where do these questions come from, first of all? Where do they originate in you? I want you to see very clearly the absurdity of asking these questions. It is essential to ask questions to learn the technical know-how of certain things. Somebody can help you, if something is wrong with the television, with the technical know-how. That is understood. I am not talking about that at all. But the questions which you are asking, you see, are of a different kind.

Where do you think these questions take their birth? How do they formulate themselves in you? They are all mechanical questions. What I am trying to emphasize all the time is that it is essential for you to understand how mechanical the whole thing is.

There is nobody who is asking the questions there. There is no questioner who is asking the questions there. There is an illusion that there is a questioner who is formulating these questions and throwing them at somebody and expecting somebody to answer them.

The answers that you get really are not the answers, because the questions persist in spite of the answers you think the other chap is giving you. The question is still there. This answer, which you think is the answer (satisfactory or otherwise), is really not the answer. If it were, the question should go once and for all. All questions are variations of the same question. You already have the answer, and all these questions are the questions that are not interested in getting any answers. The answer, if there is any to that question, should destroy the answer you already have. There is no questioner there. If the answer goes, along with the question, the questioner — non-existing questioner — also has to go. I don't know if I make myself clear.

Do you have any question which you can call your own? If you can come out with a question which you can call your own, a question that has never, never been asked before, then there is meaning in talking things over. Then you don't have to sit and ask anybody those questions, because such questions don't exist at all. A question which you can call your own, has never been asked before. All the answers are there for those questions. You probably do not realize that the questions which you are asking are born out of the answers you already have, and that they are not your answers at all. The answers have been put in there.

So why are you asking these questions, why are you not satisfied with the answers that are already there? That is my question. Why? If you are satisfied, yes, it's alright, you see. [Then you would say] "I don't want any answers." Still, the question is there inside of you. Whether you go and ask somebody or expect an answer from some wise man, it is still there. Why is it there? What happens if the question comes to an end? You come to an end. You are nothing but the answers. That's all that I am saying. If you understand that there

41

is no questioner who is asking the questions, the answer that is there is in great jeopardy. That is why it does not want any answer. The answer is the end of that answer you have, which is not yours.

So, what the hell if it is gone. The answers you have are already dead, they have been given by dead persons. Anybody who repeats those answers is a dead person. A living person cannot give any answer to those questions, because any answer that you get from anybody is a dead answer because the question is a dead question. That's the reason why I am not giving any answer to you at all. You are living in a world of dead ideas.

All the thoughts are dead, they are not living. You cannot invest them with life. That's what you are trying to do all the time: you invest them with emotions. But they are not living things. They can never touch anything living. The spiritual and psychological problems you think you have are really living problems.

So, the solutions that you have are not adequate enough to handle the living problems. They are good enough to discuss in a classroom or in some sort of question and answer ritual — repeating the same old dead ideas — but those things can never, never touch anything living, because the living thing will burn out the whole thing completely and totally.

So you are not going to touch anything living at any time. You are not looking at anything; you are not in contact with anything living, as long as you use your thoughts to understand and experience anything. When that is not there, there is no need for you to understand and experience anything. Anything you experience only gathers momentum — adds to that — that's all. There is nothing that you can call your own.

I have no questions of any kind. How come you have so many questions? I am not giving any answers. I repeat this same point day after day, day after day. Whether you understand it or not is of no importance to me.

What exactly do people mean when they talk of consciousness? There is no such thing as unconsciousness. Medical technology can find the reason why a particular individual is unconscious, but the individual who is unconscious has no way of knowing that he is unconscious. When he comes out of that unconscious state, he becomes conscious. So do you think you are conscious now? Do you think you are awake? Do you think you are alive?

It is your thinking that makes you feel that you are alive, that you are conscious. That is possible only when the knowledge you have about things is in operation. You have no way of knowing or finding out whether you are alive or dead. In that sense, there is no death at all, because you are not alive. You become conscious of things only when the knowledge is in operation. When the knowledge is absent, whether the person is dead or alive is of no importance to this movement of thought which comes to an end before what we call "death" takes place.

So, it really doesn't matter whether one is alive or dead. Of course, it does matter to one who considers that being alive is very important, and those who are involved with that individual, but you have no way of finding out whether you are alive or dead, or whether you are conscious or not. You become conscious only through the help of thought, but unfortunately it is there all the time. So, the suggestion that it is not possible to experience anything makes no sense to you at all, because you have no reference point there when this movement is absent. When this movement is absent, all those questions about consciousness are not there. That is what I mean when I say that the questions are absent.

How can you bring about a change in consciousness which has no limits, which has no boundaries, which has no frontiers. They can spend millions and millions and millions of dollars and do every kind of research to find the seat of human consciousness, but there is no such thing as the seat of human consciousness at all. You can try — and they are going to spend billions of dollars to try to find out — but the chances of their succeeding in that are impossible. There is no such thing as a seat, located in any particular individual. What is there is a thought.

Whenever a thought takes its birth, you have created an entity or a point, and in reference to that point you are experiencing things. So, when the thought is not there, is it possible for you to experience anything or relate anything to a non-existing thing here?

Every time a thought is born, you are born. Thought in its very nature is a sharp blade, and once it is gone, that's the end of it. That is probably what the traditions meant by rebirth — death and birth and death and birth. It is not that this particular entity, which is non-existing even while you are living, takes a series of births. The ending of births and deaths is the state that they are talking about.

But that state cannot be described in terms of bliss, beatitude, love, compassion and all that poetic nonsense and romantic stuff, because you have no way of experiencing what is there between these two thoughts.

The world you experience around you is also from that point of view. There must be a point and it is this point that creates the space. If this point is not there, there is no space. So, anything you experience from this point is an illusion.

Not that the world is an illusion. The world is not an illusion, but anything you experience in relationship to this point, which itself is illusory, is bound to be an illusion, that's all.

The Sanskrit word "maya" does not mean illusion in the same sense in which the English word is used. "Maya" means to measure. You cannot measure anything unless you have a point. So, if the center is absent, there is no circumference at all. That is pure and simple basic arithmetic.

This point has no continuity. It comes into being in response to the demands of the situation. The demands of the situation create this point. The subject does not exist there. It is the object that creates the subject. This runs counter to the whole philosophical thinking of India. The subject comes and goes and comes and goes in response to the things that are happening there. It is the object that creates the subject and not the subject that creates the object. This is a simple physiological phenomenon which can be tested. For example, if there is no object there, there is no subject here. What creates the subject is the object.

There is light. If the light is not there you have no way of looking at anything. The light falls on that object and the reflection of that light activates the optic nerves, which in turn activate the memory cells. When the memory cells are activated, all the knowledge you have about that object comes into cooperation. It is that process which is happening there that has created the subject. And the subject is the knowledge you have about it. The word "microphone" is the eye. There is nothing there other than the word microphone. When you reduce it to that you feel the absurdity of talking about the self — the lower self, the higher self and self knowing, self-knowledge, knowing from moment to moment is absolute rubbish, balderdash! You can indulge in such absolute nonsense and build up philosophical theories, but there is no subject there at all at any time. There is no subject creating the object.

So, not only the "I" but all the physical sensations are involved in this. Sound, the olfactory nerves, smell, and the sense of touch, the operation of any one of these sensations necessarily creates the subject. It's not one continuous subject which is gathering all these experiences and piling them up together, and then saying "This is me," but everything is discontinuous, disconnected. The sound is one, the physical seeing is one, the smelling is one. (Unfortunately man, they say, has developed 4,000 olfactory nuances which are worthless for the purpose of the survival of the living organism).

So, the sense of touch means the vibration of the sound, which creates the subject there. So it comes and goes, comes and goes, comes and goes. There is no permanent entity there at all. What is there (what you call "I") is only a first person singular pronoun. Nothing else. If you don't want to use that word "I" to prove that you are a man without "I", it is your privilege. That's all that is there. There is no permanent entity there at all.

While you are living, the knowledge that is there does not belong to you. So why are you concerned as to what will happen after what you call "you" is gone? The physical body is functioning from moment to moment because that is the way the sensory perceptions are. To talk of living from moment to moment, by creating a thought induced state of mind, has no meaning to me except in terms of the physical functioning of the body.

When thought is not there all the time, what is there is living from moment to moment. It's all frames, millions and millions and millions of frames, to put it in the language of film. There is no continuity there, there is no movement there. Thought can never, never capture the movement. It is only when you invest the thought with motion, you try to capture the movement, but actually thought can never capture any movement that is there around you.

The movement of life is the movement of life out there and here. They are together always.

So, thought is essential only for the survival of this living organism. When it is necessary, it is there. When it is not necessary, the question whether it is there or not is of no importance at all. So, you cannot talk of that state in poetic, romantic language.

If there is one [a person in that state], he won't be hiding somewhere. He will be there shining like the star. You can't keep such people under a bushel. To be an individual is not an easy thing, you see. That means you are very ordinary. It is very difficult to be ordinary, you know. You want to be something other than what you are. To be yourself is very easy, you don't have to do a thing. No effort is necessary. You don't have to exercise will, you don't have to do anything to be yourself. But to be something other than what you are, you have to do a lot of things.

Part II

I Cannot Create the Hunger in You

Q : I don't know if what happened to me one day was the same or not the same, I don't care. But I was really afraid of dying, and also of not being able to breath any more. As soon as I feel something coming up like that, I am scared to death.

U.G.: Yes. That prevented the possibility of the physical body going through the process of actual physical dying. The body has to go through it because every thought that everybody felt before you, every experience that everybody experienced before you, every feeling that everybody felt before you — all that is part of your being.

So, you can't come into your own unless the whole thing is completely and totally flushed out (if I may use that word), out of your system. That is something which you cannot do, or make happen with any effort or volition of your own. So, when the time comes, you may not have asked for it. You will never ask for the end of you as you know yourself, as you experience yourself. Sometimes it does happen, you see. So the fear of something coming to an end, the fear of what you know as your self and as you experience yourself, prevented the possibility of whole thing snapping out there. If you were lucky enough that would have happened and the whole thing would have fallen into its natural rhythm which is discontinuous and disconnected.

You see that is the way the thought functions. There is no continuity of thought. The only way it can maintain its continuity is through the constant demand for experiencing the same thing over and over and over again. So, what is there is the knowledge you have about yourself and about the world around you. The world around you is not quite different from the world you have created for yourself inside of you. What you are frightened of (not you, but that movement of thought), is the continuity coming to an end.

Q: When I was two years old I dreamt that I couldn't get air. So, I think that's an excuse.

U.G.: True, but it is not an easy thing, you know, to go through that. The whole of your energy, everything that is there is being drawn into something like a vacuum cleaner. There is a tremendous effort on your part to prevent the whole thing from being sucked into a vacuum. That's a very frightening situation. So the fear is the protective mechanism.

Q: I see.

U.G.: Physical fear is altogether different. It is very simple. It is there only for the survival of the living organism. [It operates] through your thinking and through the experiences you have built on the foundation of that physical fear (which is essential for survival) — what you call psychological fear, the fear of what you know coming to an end.

The body knows that it is immortal. I very deliberately use the word immortal because nothing there comes to an end. When what you call clinical death takes place, the body breaks itself into its constituent elements. That's all that happens. It may not reconstitute again and create the same body, which you think is yours, but when it breaks itself into its constituent elements, it provides the basis for the continuity of life. It may not be of any consolation to the individual who is dying, but this body becomes food for the millions and millions of bacteria. So, even assuming for a moment that if you resort to cremation, as they do in some countries, wherever you dump the ashes, the carbon which is the end result of the burned body, provides the basis for some tiny little flower coming out of the earth. So, nothing here is lost.

When there is an actual physical danger, the danger of the extinction of your physical body (which you think is yours), then everything that it has as its resource gets thrown into that situation and tries to survive in that particular moment.

Have you ever noticed that when there is a real physical danger your thinking mechanism is never there to help you? Never there. So you can plan ahead for every possible situation and be prepared to meet every kind of situation in your life, but actually when there is a physical danger, all your planning and all that you have thought about to be prepared to meet every kind of danger and every kind of situation, is just not there. The body has to fall back on its own resources. If for some reason it cannot renew itself and survive in that particular situation, it goes merrily and gracefully. It knows that nothing is lost.

This living organism is not interested in its continuity in terms of years. This is functioning from moment to moment. The sensory perceptions function from moment to moment. There is no continuity in your physical seeing, there is no continuity in your physical hearing, there is no continuity in your smelling, there is no continuity when you eat something, there is no continuity in the sense of touch — they are all disconnected and disjointed.

But thought in its interest to maintain itself, and to continue without any interruption, demands these experiences all the time. That is the only way it can maintain its continuity. The body functions in a completely different way; and it is not interested in the activity of the thought. The only thought that is necessary for this body is the thought that it has to use for the survival of the living organism.

Even if you do not feed this body, it is not concerned about that. It has certain resources which you have built up through years of eating. It falls back and lives on them, and when they are finished, it goes. So, for a day or two you will feel the hunger tantrums, at the same time that you usually eat, but the body is not really concerned whether you feed it or not.

At the same time it is foolish and perverse not to feed the body, hoping that you will attain some spiritual goals. That's what they do in India, they put the body through all kinds of stresses and strains — torture it — because they feel that through this endurance they will be able to achieve whatever their spiritual goals may be.

There is nothing that you can do to make that happen through any will of yours, through any effort of yours, through any volition of yours. That is the reason why I always maintain that if this kind of a thing happens, it is not something mysterious. The thought falls into its natural rhythm of discontinuous and disconnected functioning. That's all, that's all that is there.

[Then] Thought will be in harmony with the sensory perceptions and the activity of the senses. There is no conflict there, there is no struggle there, there is no pain there. There is a harmonious relationship between the two [thought and body]. Whenever there is a need for thought, it is always there to act. The action that this body is interested in is only the action that is essential for the survival of the living organism.

The body is not interested in any ideas you have about your religious or material goals. It is not at all interested. There is always a constant battle between these two things [thought and the body].

Thought is not something mysterious. It is what the culture has put in there, which is, of course, society. They are not different — culture and society. Society is interested in its continuity and permanence. It is interested in the status quo. It is always maintaining that status quo. That is where thought is helpful for the society. Society says, "If you don't act that way, if you don't think that way you will become anti-social because all your actions will become thoughtless, impulsive actions." It is interested in channeling every thought of yours in that particular direction which maintains the status quo. That is why there is basically, essentially and fundamentally a conflict between these two [society and the individual]. Culture has been adopted and accepted as a means of survival, that's all.

It [culture] has a momentum of its own, totally unrelated to it [the survival of the body]. As long as you use that [culture], you are not an individual at all. You can become an individual only when you break away from the totality of that wisdom.

There's no such thing as your mind or my mind. Maybe there is such a thing as the "world mind" where all the cumulative knowledge and the experiences thereof are accumulated and passed on from generation to generation. We have to use that mind to function in this world sanely and intelligently. If we don't use it, as I was saying the other day, we will end up on the funny farm singing loony tunes and merry melodies. The society is interested only in fitting every individual into its framework and maintaining its continuity.

[U.G. sighs and says quietly, "I don't want to give a talk."]

I don't know if I have made myself clear. The reason why I am emphasizing the physical aspect is not with the idea of selling something, but to emphasize and express what you call enlightenment, liberation, moksha, mutation, transformation, in pure and simple physical and physiological terms. There is absolutely no religious content to it and no mystical overtones or undertones to the functioning of the body. But unfortunately, for centuries they have interpreted the whole thing in religious terms and that has created misery for us all. The more you try to revive or push it through the backdoor, when there is no interest in the religious life, you are only adding more and more to the misery.

I am not interested in propagating this. This is not something which you can make happen, nor is it possible for me to create that hunger which is essential to understand anything. I repeat this over and over again, but repetition has its own charm.

You are assuming that you are hungering for spiritual attainments and you are reaching out for your goals. Naturally, there are so many people in the market place — all these saints, selling all kinds of shoddy goods. For whatever reason they are doing it, it's not our concern, but they are doing it.

They say it is for the welfare of mankind and that they do it out of compassion for mankind and all that kind of thing. All that is bullshit anyway. What I am trying to say is that you are satisfied with the crumbs they throw at you. And they promise that one day they are going to deliver to you a full loaf of bread. That is just a promise. They cannot deliver the goods at all. They just don't have it. They can only cut it into pieces and distribute it to the people.

What I am saying is, that hunger has got to burn itself up. Every day I am saying the same thing but using different words, you see, putting these things in different ways. That's all that I can do. My vocabulary is very, very limited, so I have to use the same words again and again and emphasize the same thing all over again to point out that the hunger has to burn itself up.

There is no use feeding yourself with all kinds of junk food. There is no use waiting for something to happen to satisfy your hunger. There is no point in satisfying that hunger. The hunger has to burn itself up — literally it has to burn itself out.

Even physical hunger has to burn itself out so that a physical death can take place. Actual dehydration of the body takes place. Thank god the physical body has certain things to protect itself when the physical dehydration takes place. I don't know if you have meditated for hours and hours: the whole body reaches a point where dehydration takes place. Then you have these life-savers there in your body — the saliva — there is a profuse saliva coming out to quench your thirst and save you in that particular situation when you push this body to do certain things — meditation, yoga, all kinds of things people do (overdo these things).

There is one thing that I am emphasizing all the time: it is not because of what you do or what you do not do that this kind of a thing happens. And why it happens to one individual and not another — there is no answer to that question. I assure you that it is not [going to happen to] the man who has prepared himself, or purified himself (for whatever reason) to be ready to receive that kind of a thing. It is the other way around. It hits. But it hits at random. That is the way nature operates. Lightning hits you somewhere. It is not interested in whether it is hitting a tree that is blooming or if it has fruits and is helping the people by providing shade, etc. It just strikes at random. In exactly the same way it happens to a particular individual, and that happening is acausal. It has no cause.

There are so many things happening in nature which cannot be attributed to any particular cause. So, your interest in studying the lives or the biography of some of those people whom you think were enlightened, or godmen or some such thing, is to find a clue as to how it happened to them, so that you can use whatever technique they used and make the same thing happen to you. That is your interest. Those people are giving you some techniques, some system, some methods which don't work at all. They create the hope that somehow, through some miracle, one day it is going to happen to you. But it will never happen.

I have said my piece. And I have to repeat this again and come to it from ten different angles, depending upon the nature of the questions which you throw at me.

But, as I said yesterday, all questions are exactly the same. Because the questions spring from the answers you already have, the answers given by others are not really the answers. I am not giving any answers to you. If I am foolish enough to give you the answers, you have to understand that this is the very answer which is destroying the possibility of that question disappearing. You have to take my word — I don't care if you take my word or not — that such questions never, never, never occur to me.

I have no questions of any kind except the questions I need to ask somebody, "where can I rent a car?" "What is the quickest way to go to Brussels?" "Which way to Rotterdam — this road or that road?" That's all. For such questions, there are always people who can help you. But these other kinds of questions have no answers.

When it dawns on you that such questions have no answers, and that those questions spring from the answers you already have, that situation is the complete and total blasting of the answers that you have. That is something which you cannot make happen. It is not in your hands.

So, you think the situation is hopeless, but it is not hopeless. The hope is here. The hope is not there. You are waiting for something to happen tomorrow. Tomorrow NOTHING will happen!

Whatever has to happen, it has got to happen now. The possibility of that happening now is practically and well nigh impossible, because the instrument which you are using is the past. Unless the past comes to an end, there cannot be any present. And that present moment is something which cannot be captured by you, cannot be experienced by you. Even assuming for a moment that the past has come to an end, you have no way of knowing that it has come to an end. Then there is no future for you at all. Maybe tomorrow you will be the boss of your company, or the school teacher will become the head of the institution, and the professor will become the dean — that possibility is there, but you have to put in a lot of struggle and that takes time. You are applying the same technique to realize whatever you are interested in [spiritual goals] and so it [your mind] puts it out there as a goal in the future. It has produced tremendous results in this world. So, how can that instrument not be the instrument to achieve your spiritual goals? You have tried, you have done everything possible — even those of you who are burning with hunger to find it — but it's impossible.

In India everybody has tried this — you wouldn't believe it — not one was lucky enough. Whenever such a thing has happened, it happened to those people who had given up completely and totally all their search. That is an absolute requisite for that kind of a thing. The whole movement has to slow down and come to a stop. But anything you do to make it stop is only adding momentum to it. That's really the crux of the problem.

What you are interested in doesn't exist. It's your own imagination, based upon the knowledge you have about those things. And so, there is nothing that you can do about it. You are chasing something that does not exist at all. I can say that until the cows return home — I don't know when they return home here — or till kingdom come — but that kingdom will never come. So, you keep on going, hoping that somehow you will find some way of achieving your goals. Your interest in attaining that for the purpose of solving your day to day problems is a farfetched idea because that cannot be of any help to you to solve your problems. "If I had that enlightenment I would be able to solve all my problems."

You cannot have all that and enlightenment. When that comes, it wipes out everything! You want all this and heaven too. Not a chance! That is something which cannot be made to happen through your effort or through the grace of anybody, through the help of even a god walking on the face of this earth claiming that he has specially descended from wherever (from whatever heavens) for your sake and for the sake of mankind — that is just absolute gibberish. Nobody can help you. Help you to achieve what? That is the question, you see.

As long as your goal is there, these persons, their promises and their techniques will look very, very attractive to you. They go together. There is not anything you must do. Anyway, you are already doing [many things]. Can you be without doing anything? You can't be without doing anything. Unfortunately you are doing something, and that doing has got to come to an end. In order to bring that doing to an end, you are doing something else. That is really the crux of the problem. That's the situation in which you find yourself. That's all that I can say. I point out the absurdity of what you are doing.

As I said yesterday, what brings you here will certainly take you somewhere else. You have nothing to get here, you will not get anything here. Not that I want to keep anything for myself; you can take anything you want. I have nothing to give you. I am not anything that you are not. You think that I am something different. The thought that I am different from others never enters my head.

Never. Whenever they ask questions I feel, "Why are these people asking these questions? How can I make them see?" I still have some trace of illusion. Maybe I can try. But even that "try" has no meaning to me. There's nothing that I can do about it.

There is nothing to get. Nothing to give and nothing to get. That is the situation. In the material world, yes. We have a lot of things. There is always somebody who can help you with the knowledge, with the money, with so many things in the world. But here in this field there is nothing to give and nothing to get. As long as you want you can be certain you ain't got a chance. You see, wanting implies that you are going to set your thinking in motion to achieve your goal. It is not a question of achieving your goal, but it is a question of this movement coming to an end here. The only thing that you can do is to set in motion this movement of thought in the direction of achieving that. How are you going to achieve this impossible task?

Wanting and thinking — they always go together. I am not for a moment suggesting that you should suppress all your wants, or free yourself from all your wants, and control all your wants. Not at all. That's the religious game. If you want anything, the one thing that you will do is to set in motion the movement of thought to achieve your goal.

Material goals, yes, but even there it's not so easy. It is such a competitive world. Not much is left for us to share. Not enough to go around. The talk of sharing with somebody is poppycock to me. There is nothing to be shared here. This is not an experience. Even assuming for a moment that this is an experience, even then it is so difficult to share with somebody else unless the other individual has some reference point within the framework of his experiencing structure. So, then you see the whole business becomes a sort of meaningless ritual — sitting and discussing these matters. That's all. It's not so easy for you to give up. Not at all.

Q: This thing happened to me when I didn't know anything about anything.

U.G.: Nothing, you see, it just happened.

Q: But I just was sitting down on the floor and it happened. I was scared to death about it.

U.G.: That's all right. Now you want that to happen again? No? Thank god. Your spiritual search ends that way. There is no other way. It is not that I am trying to frighten you, but how do you expect that to happen? That is how all those people who have taken drugs experience all kinds of things. Those who have not heard of anything of this kind certainly experience so many things and that puts them on this merry-go-round. India has any number of techniques, systems, and methods to give you every kind of experience you want. That is why they are doing a tremendously roaring business.

Q: But it didn't even come in my head as it did with meditation, or with this or with that, because it was something different.

U.G.: It happened, such things happen. Some extraordinary experiences. People experience without knowing, without asking for that [experience]. Without doing any such things. This was a frightening experience for you — but you want to make other spiritual experiences happen again and again and again. Anything you

61

make happen has no meaning at all. Then you will want more and more of those things. And then, when you succeed in having more and more of those things, you will demand some kind of a permanent situation, permanent happiness, permanent bliss. Yet there is no such thing as permanence at all. No. Probably your experience would have resulted in bliss, who knows.

Q: Are you saying then that we are what we are already?

U.G.: You don't want to accept that fact, but you want to know what you are. That's the problem. You have no way of knowing it at all. Knowing what is there is impossible. That is always related to what you want to be. What you see here is the opposite of what you would like to be, what you want to be, what you ought to be, what you should be. What do you see here? You want to be happy, so you are unhappy. Wanting to be happy creates the unhappiness. What you see here is the opposite of your goal of becoming happy, of wanting to be happy. Wanting to have pleasure all the time creates the pain here. So, wanting and thinking, they always go together. They are not separate. Anything you want creates pain, because you begin to think. Wanting and thinking. If you don't want a thing in this world, there is no thinking. That does not mean thoughts are not there.

Whether you want to achieve material goals or spiritual goals it really doesn't matter. I am not saying anything against wanting. Want means the fulfillment of the want or non-fulfillment of the want is possible only through thinking.

So, the thinking has really created the problem for you. What I am suggesting is that all the problems we have cannot be solved on psychological and ethical levels. Man has tried for centuries to solve them but he has failed. What keeps him going is the hope that one day, by doing more and more of the same, he will achieve his goals. But the body, as I was saying, has a way of resolving these problems because, you see, it cannot take them. The sensitivity of the sensory perceptions is destroyed by whatever you are doing to free yourself from whatever you want to be free from. It is destroying the sensitivity of the nervous system here.

The nervous system has to be very alert for the survival of this living organism. It has to be very sensitive. Your sensory perceptions have to be very sensitive. Instead of allowing them to be sensitive, you have invented what is called the "sensitivity" of your feelings, the sensitivity of your mind, the sensitivity towards every living thing around you, sensitivity to the feelings of everybody that is there. And this has created a neurological problem. So all the problems are neurological. Not psychological and not ethical. That's the problem of the society.

Society is interested in the status quo, it doesn't want to change. The only way it can maintain the status quo or the continuity is through this demand — the demand that everybody should fit into this structure. Whereas every individual is unique, physically speaking. Nature is creating something unique all the time. It is not interested in a perfect man; it is not interested in a religious man.

We have placed before man the goal or the ideal of a perfect man, a truly religious man. So anything you do to reach that goal of perfection is destroying the sensitivity of this body. It is creating violence here. It [the body] is not interested in that.

Whatever the dead man experiences — self-awareness, self-consciousness — he has sown the seeds of the total destruction of man. All religions have come out of that divisive consciousness

63

in man. All the teachings of those teachers will inevitably destroy mankind. There is no point in reviving all those things and starting revivalistic movements. That is dead, finished.

Anything that is born out of this division in your consciousness is destructive, is violence. It is so because it is trying to protect not this living organism, not life, but the continuity of thought. And through that it can maintain the status quo of your culture, or whatever you want to call it, the society. The problems are neurological. If you give a chance to the body it will handle all those problems. But if you try to solve them on a psychological level or on an ethical level, you are not going to succeed.

Q: What do you mean by "giving a chance to the body?"

U.G.: Where is anger? In your stomach you feel it, you see. In the base here. If you beat your husband or wife or neighbor, or beat the pillows, you are not going to solve the problem. It is already absorbed. You are only enriching these therapists who are making money out of that. You hit your wife, husband, anybody you want and that's all that you can do, nothing else. But still it is the function of the body to handle that and absorb it. It is in here. It is something real there for the body. It doesn't want this anger, because it is destroying the sensitivity of the nervous system. So, it is absorbing the whole thing and you don't have to do a thing.

Any energy that you create through this thinking is destructive for this body. That energy cannot be separated from life here. It is one continuous movement. So, all the energies you experience as a result of playing with all those things are not of any interest to the smooth functioning of this living organism.

They are disturbing the harmonious functioning of this body — a very, very peaceful thing.

The peace there is not this inane dead silence you experience. It's like a volcano erupting all the time. That is the silence, that is peace. The blood is flowing through your veins like a river. If you tried to magnify the sound of the flow of your blood you will be surprised — it's like the roar of the ocean. If you put yourself in a sound proof room you will not survive even for five minutes. You will go crazy, because you can't bear the noises that are there in you. The sound of the beat of your heart is something which you cannot take. You love to surround yourself with all these sounds and then you create some funny experience called the "experience of the silent mind," which is ridiculous. Absurd. That is the silence that is there — the roar — the roar of an ocean. The roaring of the flow of blood. That is all that it [the body] is interested in, not your state of mind nor the experience of the silent mind. It is not interested in your practice of virtues nor in the practice of your silences. The body has no interest in your moral dilemma or whatever you want to call it. It's not interested in your virtues or vices. As long as you practice virtues, so long you will remain a man of vice. They go together. If you are lucky enough to be free from this pursuit of virtue, as a goal, along with it the vice also goes out of your system. You will not remain a man of vice. You will remain a man of violence as long as you follow some idea of becoming a non-violent, kind, soft, gentle person. A kind man, a man who is practicing kindness, a man who is practicing virtues is really a menace. Not the [so-called] violent man.

Somewhere along the line, culture has put the whole thing on the wrong track by placing before man the ideal of a perfect man

— the ideal of a truly religious man. The religious experience is born out of this division in his consciousness, which is not its nature.

Luckily animals don't have this division in their consciousness, except the division that is essential for their survival. Man is worse than an animal. He has no doubt succeeded in putting man on the moon. Probably he will put men on every planet, but that achievement is of no interest to this body. That achievement is moving in the direction of progressively destroying everything, because anything that is born out of thought is destructive. Not only destructive to the body, but destructive, progressively moving in the direction of destroying everything that man has built for himself.

Q: Anything is destructive if you are hungry.

U.G.: Your body is not interested in your hunger after one day. You will be surprised if you don't feed the body. Feeding your body is your own problem. Maybe for one or two days you will feel the hunger tantrums.

Q: Well if you stop eating you'll eventually die.

U.G.: So what. The body doesn't die. It changes its form, shape, breaks itself into its constituent elements. It is not interested in that. For the body there is no death. For your thinking there is a death, because it does not want to come to an end. For thought there is a death. So, because it does not want to face that situation, it has created the life after, the lives to come. But this body is immortal in its nature, because it is part of life.

Q: Even when the body is underground and disintegrating?

U.G.: So what. There are so many other forms of life surviving on that body. It is of no consolation to you, but all those germs will have a heyday on your body. A feast day. A big feast. If you leave the body there in the streets, you will be surprised. They will all have a field day, a feast. You will be doing great a service. Not for mankind, but for organisms of different kinds.

Q: It is also not advisable to be a vegetarian?

U.G.: Ah, well. [He sighs wearily]

Q: Here we go again.

U.G.: Vegetarianism for what? For some spiritual goals? One form of life lives off another. That's a fact, whether you like it or not. If tigers practiced vegetarianism — he says [pointing to the questioner] his cat is a vegetarian cat, it doesn't kill a fly. Because of its association with vegetarians it has become vegetarian. For health reasons maybe one should. I don't know, I don't see any adequate reason why one should be a vegetarian. Your body is not going to be any more pure than the meat eating body. You go to India, [you observe that] those that have been vegetarians, they are not kind, they are not peaceful. So it has nothing to do [with spirituality] — what you put in there is not really the problem.

Q: What about aggression which is caused by eating meat.

U.G.: Vegetarians are more aggressive than meat-eaters. You will be surprised. Read the history of India — bloodshed, massacres, assassination — all in the name of religion.

That's why I am emphasizing that the teachers and the teachings are responsible for this mess in this world. All those messiahs have created nothing but a mess in this world. And the politicians are the inheritors of that culture. There is no use blaming them and calling them corrupt. They were corrupted.

The man who taught love was corrupt because he created division in his consciousness. The man who spoke of "Love thy neighbor as thyself" was responsible for this horror in the world today. Don't exonerate those teachers. Their teachings have created nothing but mess in this world, progressively moving in the direction of destroying not only man, but every species on this planet today.

It came out of that [ideal of love]. It's not the scientists and politicians that are responsible. They have this power in their hands, and they are going to use it — there are enough lunatics in this world who will press the button. But it [violence] originated where?

Religion is not going to save man, neither will atheism, nor communism, nor any of those systems. You can't put them on a pedestal and say that they should be exonerated. Not only the teaching but the teachers themselves have sown the seeds of this violence that we have in this world. The man who talked of love is responsible, because love and hate go together. So how can you exonerate them. Don't blame the followers, the followers have come out of that teaching. That's history, not my personal opinion.

Talk of love is one of the most absurd things. There must be two [for there to be love]. Wherever there is a division there is this destruction. Kindness needs two — you are kind to somebody, or you are kind to yourself. There is a division there in your consciousness. Anything that is born out of that division is a protective mechanism, and in the long run it is destructive.

Thought is trying to protect itself. That is why it is interested in continuity. The body is not interested in protecting itself. Whatever intelligence is necessary for the survival of the body is already there.

The jungle we have created through our organization needs that intellect, the intellect that we have acquired through our studies, through our culture, through the whole lot. It has a parallel existence of its own and it is interested in a different kind of survival, because there is no end to the life here. This is only an expression of the life. If you and I go, the life [still] goes on. Those lights go off, but the electricity continues. Something else will come. It is not interested in man. Man, unfortunately, has such destructive powers, which have originated from the experience of man (his self-awareness).

So the talk of wanting to look at himself, to understand himself, is a divisive movement in man, born out of that self-awareness. That's the foundation upon which the whole psychological structure is built.

Q: But how can we get rid of that divisive thinking?

U.G.: You can't. It's not in your hands. Anything you do adds momentum to that. So do you want that to come to an end? No.

Q: I once felt an enormous unity . . .

U.G.: There is a disturbance in the metabolism of the body brought about through drugs or through meditation or through any of those systems and techniques man has invented. "You can experience the oneness of life, and unity of life." [mocking us] Look at India, which preaches the unity of life and the oneness of life, there you have an example. They are all great metaphysicians, philosophers, everlastingly discussing these things. But it doesn't operate in the lives of the people.

Q: The understanding that there is that dualism, the coming of that understanding . . .

U.G.: Understanding is dualism. If that division is not there, there is nothing to understand. So the instrument which you are using to understand something is the only instrument you have. There is no other instrument. You can talk of intuition, you can talk of a thousand other things. They are all sensitized thoughts. Intuition is nothing but a sensitized thought — but still it is a thought. So anything you understand through the help of that instrument has not helped you to understand anything. That is not the instrument, and there is no other instrument. If that is the case, is there anything to understand. Your understanding of anything is only for the purpose of changing what is there. Whatever is there, you want to change. You want to bring about a change in the structure of your thinking, so, you begin to think differently and you begin to experience differently. But basically there is no change there.

70

Your wanting to understand anything is only for the purpose of bringing about a change there, and at the same time you do not want the change. That has created the neurotic situation in man, wanting two things, change and no change. That is the conflict that is there all the time.

Q: Possibly we have to see that conflict.

U.G.: The seeing itself is a divisive movement. There are two things. You know, the Indians are past masters in this game — the seer and the seen, the observer and the observed. They are great experts in this kind of a game. But what is there to see? Who is it that is seeing? Are there two things? What do you do when you see? You are back again to the same thought.

It is absurd to ask yourself the question "Who am I?" Why do you ask that question? That means there is some other "I" there that you want to know. That question has no meaning to me at all. The very fact that you ask that question implies that there are two things. The "I" you know, and there is another "I" the nature of which you do not know. The question "who am I" implies that there is some other I, the nature of which you really do not know and you want to know. I don't know if I make myself clear. Do you know anything about yourself, first of all. What do you know? Tell me. Hmm?

Q: What he knows.

U.G.: What he has been told: where he lives, what his name is, how much money he is drawing every month, his telephone number, people he has met, how many experiences he has gathered during the course of his 30 years, and all the books he has read. That's all that he can tell you. He can repeat mechanically, all the information he has gathered and all the experiences he has collected. And so, that is all that is there. Why are you dissatisfied with it, and why are you searching for something other than that? Can you tell me something about yourself other than the information that you have gathered, what you know?

Q: What I found there is not the answer. Otherwise the questions would not persist.

U.G.: What did you find there?

Q: Just knowledge.

U.G.: So that question, that idiotic question, is born out of the knowledge you already have. It is the knowledge that is there that has thrown out [asked] this question, "Who am I." So you want to know, and through that knowing the knowledge you have gathers momentum. You are adding more and more and more [to the knowledge]. If there is anything to be known there, all you know should come to an end. So, by this pursuit or the demand to get an answer for that question, you are adding more and more to the knowledge.

So, don't you see the absurdity of the question, "Who am I?" It doesn't matter who suggested that, who threw that question at you, who recommended that question. There is nothing there to know. What is there is all that you know. When that is not there, there is no need for you to know anything, and there is no way of knowing anything about what is there.

72

Q: But "Who am I" is not really a question. "Who am I" is a pointer.

U.G.: Yes. Where does the point lead you? All right, if it is a pointer, what do you do? You stay put there and instead of following that, you suck your finger. What do you do with that pointer?

Q: The pointer points to where there is nothing to be pointed. It takes you to where these are all nonsensical words.

U.G.: That's all right, the question itself is a nonsensical question.

Q: Yes. But it is only so if you use it as a question.

U.G.: All right. Even if you use it as a pointer, the very direction is wrong.

Q: It's not even a pointer.

U.G.: All right, what is it then?

Q: It shows you that you are. It shows you that I am. "I am" is the basis.

U.G.: What I am is the knowledge I have about myself.

Q: "I am" is what I am.

U.G.: But what does it mean, what I am?

Q: It doesn't mean anything . . .

U.G.: Yes.

Q: "I am" is not knowledge.

U.G.: There is nothing there, no existence there independent of the question.

Q: So it is the end of knowledge.

U.G.: So the question should end. Because the question itself — listen — the question itself is born out of the answer. Otherwise there is no place for any question of any kind. All questions are born out of the answers you already have. So it is idiotic even to ask a question for which you already have an answer. Because there can't be any question without an answer, the question implies that there is something about that "I" you do not know, but want to know — something other than the "I" that is already there; it implies that there is another "I" there.

Q: On a certain level, yes. You can also say if you ask a question it means that you know the answer.

U.G.: That's right. There's no question at all. There can't be any question without knowledge. All questions are born out of the answers you already have. So, that is the reason why a question of that kind, whether it is posed by yourself or somebody else, does not want an answer. The answer for any question is the end of the question. The end of the question means the end of the answer that you already have. Not only your answer, but the answers that have been accumulating for centuries must not be there. The demand for an answer to that question, on any level (there is only one level, there are no other levels), implies that the questioner does not want the knowledge to come to an end.

Q: That's true. But of course in the process of this . . .

U.G.: It has to happen now, not in the end, because there is no time. The instrument which you are using, which is this process of knowledge, does not want to come to an end. That is why it is posing the question to itself, knowing very well that the question is bound to carry on until it gets an answer.

So, this knowledge, the instrument which you are using, does not know, and cannot conceive of, the possibility of anything happening except in time, because it is born in time and it functions in time. Although it projects a state of timelessness, it is not interested in accepting the fact that nothing can happen except in the field of time. The question implies that there is a demand for an answer and that answer can come only in time. And during that time this knowledge has a chance of surviving.

Q: It's true what you say. However, the answer to the question "Who am I" does not fall in time.

U.G.: Yes. But anything that is born . . .

Q: It is only a device. I agree with you.

U.G.: That is true. Anything that is born in the field of time is time. The question is time.

Q: The question is not born in time.

U.G.: Where does it come from?

Q: It comes from "I am."

U.G.: That assumption itself is time — that "I am". Of course, it is an assumption — that there is something there other than this knowledge. What is there is only the knowledge.

Q: If, as you say, you ask questions born out of the answers you already have, do you mean that the "answers that you already have" is the same as what psychology means by the "mind."

U.G.: I don't know . . . To me there is no mind at all. The mind is the totality (it's not that I am giving a peculiar definition of mind), the totality of your experiences and the totality of your thoughts. As I was saying yesterday, there are no thoughts which you can call your own. There is no experience which you can call your own. Without knowledge you cannot have any experience. I don't know if I make myself clear. Every time you experience, through the help of this experience, the knowledge is strengthened and fortified. This is a vicious circle. It goes on and on and on. The knowledge gives you experiences and the experiences fortify the knowledge you have.

The questions which you are asking are very frivolous questions because the questions are born out of the knowledge. If there is any answer to that question, it is not necessarily your answer. All answers are the answers that have been accumulated through centuries. There is a totality of the knowledge that has been accumulated. Accumulative knowledge, accumulative experiences are all there. You are using them to communicate to yourself and to communicate to others. So, there is no such thing as your mind and my mind. But there is a mind which is the totality of all the thoughts and experiences of all that has existed up to this point.

So, any answer that anybody gives for that question should put an end to that question. The fact is that the answers given by others, the answers that you have manufactured for yourself, and the answers given by these wise men we have in the market place today and those who existed in the past, are not really the answers. Any answer I give to your question cannot be the answer to that question, because the answer should put an end to the question. If the question is shattered there, along with it all the knowledge that is responsible for that question has also got to go. The questioner is not interested in any answer, because the answer has to blow up the whole thing, not only what little you have known in this 30 or 40 years, but all that has accumulated up to that point, everything that every man thought and felt and experienced before up to the point where the question is thrown out. I don't think I make myself clear. But anyway, you see, the answer, if there is any answer, should wipe out the whole thing.

Q: I was thinking of the despair that occurs when the vacuum is on the brink of becoming a reality, or seemingly near.

U.G.: Yes, but, assuming for a moment that there is despair there (you say you are in great despair), have you given up trying to free yourself from despair? You call it despair in the same way you are using the word vacuum or emptiness. But there is no despair there.

The existentialist philosophers have built up a tremendous philosophical structure on what they call despair, religious people call it the divine despair — these are all meaningless phrases. You have never really come to grips with what you call despair, because there is only a movement in the direction of wanting somehow to free yourself from the situation which you call despair. So you don't let that despair act. That is the action that I am talking about. You are still thinking about that, you know. Where is that despair? It is not in the area of your thinking. It should be here in the framework of your body. Where is that despair you are talking about? As long as you are trying to run away, move away from the despair, there is no despair there.

Wanting to be free from despair is all that you are interested in. Because you think it is not choking you, it is not killing you. The despair should destroy this movement for freeing yourself from this. You are not giving the despair a chance to act. You are interested in finding out a solution, a way out of this impasse. That's all that is there — and you give it a name and call it "despair." You are not in despair. You don't act like a person in despair. You just talk about despair, you talk about vacuum, you talk about emptiness. It's not really emptiness. If there is emptiness, that's the action of life.

Next you will ask me "what is life?" If I define life, we are lost. What I mean by life is that which makes it possible for the whole of your being to respond. Not react, respond — respond to the stimuli around you. If there is no life there, you become a corpse. A dead corpse is still responding but in a different way. That is why you call this life. Life, in other words, is nothing but the pulse and the beat and the breath of life. That's also a definition. There is a pulse, there is breathing, there is a throb of life. It is throbbing all over, everywhere, every cell in your body is throbbing. That's all that is life. But we are not really talking about that life, because nobody can say anything about that life, except to give

78

definitions. You can call it life-force, this, that and the other, but living implies all the other problems that the so-called life creates.

There is a demand for "how." How to live. That is really the problem. The problem of all problems is how to live. And for centuries we have been brainwashed to believe that "This is how you should live." If that is not satisfactory, you find another way and call that "How to live." And it goes on and on and on and on. All that is nonsense, because it has not given you peace. There is a constant battle going on inside of you, a war going on inside of you. As long as there is a war inside of you, there isn't going to be a peaceful world at all. Even assuming for a moment that war has come to an end, and you are at peace with yourself, that will not change anything, because, you see, a man who is at peace with himself will be a threat to his neighbor. So, there is a danger he will liquidate you.

The important problem is, can you bring this war to an end within yourself. Is there any way? All the solutions that you have, are the ones that are responsible for this battle — that is, "How to live." The "how" has to go. Then you ask me, "How can that 'how' go?" "Can you help me?"

First of all, you are not sure of that. You have not even come to that point of despair. Only then can you deal with the despair. As long as you are running in the direction of wanting to be free from despair, it is just not possible for you to handle that despair. There may be a hundred and fifty solutions, but you can't try all of them. Obviously all that you have tried has failed, and so you say you are in despair. That despair will act.

What is the action? That action can never be within the framework of your thinking. Any action that is within the framework or the product of your thinking, will inevitably create despair. It may give you a reason or a certain experience for a while, but you always demand more and more and more of the same. This keeps the whole thing going, and that gives you hope.

The hope is here, and you say the situation is hopeless. The situation is not hopeless. The hope is here now because, as you say, the despair is there. And so you hope to resolve that, to solve that, to handle that, to come to grips with it, and find out if there is any way of freeing yourself from the despair. Instead of letting that despair act, you are running away from it and still trying to find out if there is any way that you can be free from despair.

That applies to all the situations in life. Either you are stuck with your frustration, which is despair, or something else. What do you want to do in such a situation? You have to find the solution for yourself. If I give you another solution it will be like the hundreds of solutions that you already have. You will add this to your list of solutions. This is not going to help you to solve your problem. It makes it more difficult. Now you have one more solution. If there is any solution, that solution has to come from that which you are trying to be free from, and not from any outside agency. That action is something extraordinary.

If once that problem of despair is solved, all the others are solved, because every other problem is a variation of the same. So you never want to solve the problem. You are more interested in solutions. That's why I am repeating the same thing over and over in ten different ways. (My vocabulary is limited so I have to use the same words. You can increase your vocabulary and find new phrases, but it doesn't serve any purpose).

The instrument which you are using, which is thinking, can never accept the fact that these problems can be solved here and now, because it has taken so much time for you to be what you are. You are living in a world of your experiences and it has taken so many years for you to be what you are. That is the only instrument you have. You have no other way of handling these problems. That mechanism cannot conceive of the possibility of finding out the solution here and now. It is always interested in pushing it further and further and further away. There is always tomorrow. There is always this time.

Because this functions in the field of time, it cannot conceive of the possibility of anything else happening, of any action other than the action in the field of time. This is not metaphysics that I am discussing.

The solution, if there is any, has to be here and now. If you are hungry, hunger must be satisfied. If the hunger cannot be satisfied, it will burn you up. This is a frightening situation for you, so you are satisfied with the crumbs which are the solutions that people throw at you. You are waiting for somebody to give you a full loaf of bread or some miracle man to multiply the loaves of bread.

But that's not going to happen. There is no real hunger there. You don't want to solve this problem, because then you will find yourself without a problem. So, that which gives you strength and energy is trying to solve your problem. When once you achieve your goal, what you have there is frustration.

Even in the sex act (which is so powerful in the life of an individual), it is the preparation, it is the build up, it is the tension that is the attractive part of it. When once the tension is built up there, this

81

body is demanding release from the tension which you call pleasure — release. It wants to be released from the tension which you have built up. It wants a release, which you call the orgasm, or whatever you want to call it. So there is a tremendous relief.

So what is there now? A vacuum. In exactly the same way, all actions are functioning in the same field. You build up, build up, build up tension, and then you see it [the tension] demands a release.

The other day I was reading an article in *Playboy*. "How to Keep The Orgasm Going for Half An Hour." My god! They are doing experiments. You know they have succeeded. There was one doctor in California who has succeeded through artificial means, with the help of gadgets. They have established that a woman can have an orgasm for half an hour. All the other specialists say it's only for a few seconds. It is the demand for the extension of that agony which you call pleasure — it is not pleasure, it's release of tension.

You work hard to achieve your goal, and once you achieve the goal you are exhausted, you are finished, the charm is lost for you. Working for it, building up all these tensions — that is all that you are interested in. When once you are there, it's finished for you. You have lost it. So you start all over again.

You don't want to be without any problems. You are yourself the problem. If you don't have any problems, you create problems. The end of the problem is the end of you. So these problems will remain until the end. You go, then the problems go. Seventy, eighty, ninety, a hundred years — it depends upon how long you are going to live — the hope remains. It's not a pessimistic situation, it is a realistic situation. I am not giving you any solutions. Please, for goodness sake, look at your problem, if you can. You can't separate yourself from the problem. The problem is created by the opposite of it.

Why do you feel unhappy, first of all? Why do feel this feeling of unkindness in you? Because of the goal. It is that which creates the opposite. You can see for yourself, I don't have to tell you. You are always thinking, "I should be like that, I ought to be that, I must be like that, and I am not that." It is that thought that has created the opposite of it. If that is gone, this also is gone. This man cannot be a career man. This man cannot be a sensitive man — not sensitive within the framework of your cultural mores.

This is a different kind of sensitivity. As long as you are pursuing those ideals that the society or the culture has placed before you, you will remain the opposite of it. And you hope that one day, through some miracle or through the help of somebody, some god, some guru, you will be able to resolve the problem — *not a chance!*. [U.G. shouts dramatically]

I cannot create the hunger in you. How can I create the hunger in you? If you have the hunger, you will look around and you will find that whatever is offered to you is not satisfying. If you are satisfied with the crumbs, all right. That's what the gurus are doing, throwing some crumbs for you, like they do to the dog on a leash. Humans are like animals, no different. If we accept the fact that we are not different, then there is a better chance we will act as humans.

Q: When will they act as humans?

U.G.: When man ceases to pursue the goal of a perfect man.

Part III

Nice Meeting You, and Goodbye

Q : May I ask you something?

U.G.: Yes, please.

Q: This constant change that we want to come about with our inner self, not necessarily changing the world but trying to find our inner self when we do meditation, or yoga, or whatever, why do we want this change?

U.G.: Why do you do them all?

Q: Well I try them out, I do them, and I see . . . .

U.G.: What for? Do you want to change something?

Q: That's the point, yes. Why do we want to change? What is it in us that wants this constant change? Why can't we be satisfied?

U.G.: You are dissatisfied with yourself, first of all? hmm?

Q: Not consciously . . . it's a funny thing. I feel very good, I have relatively little to complain about, and yet . . . .

U.G.: And yet you do. Do you see the paradox? You are not as contented as you say you are, as satisfied as you say you are.

Q: That's right.

U.G.: Something there determines that all is not right. That's why, you want to bring about a change. And who is responsible for that demand to change? That is what I am saying: culture, society, has placed the demand before you that you should be like that, you ought to be like that. You understand? So you have accepted that as a model for yourself.

Q: But I don't feel that I have an image of a person or a thing that I am striving for. What I am trying to find out is, is there something more inside?

U.G.: No. The demand for more . . .

Q: The inner thing . . .

U.G.: There is no inner and outer. What I am trying to say is that there is a feeling, there is a demand, that there is something more interesting that you can do with yourself, more meaningful, more. purposeful than your existence is today. That is the demand, you see. That is why there is this restlessness. You become restless because of this drive in you, which is put in there by the society or culture, that makes you feel that there is something more interesting, more meaningful, more purposeful, that your life can be than what it is today.

Q: And the naturalness of your self doesn't exist?

U.G.: No.

Q: It's just words that society has put together?

U.G.: Exactly, your naturalness is destroyed by that demand which is put in there by the culture. So, then your life looks meaningless to you if that is all that you can do. You have tried to fill in that boredom with everything possible . . . . now you have all these new gimmicks — yoga, meditation, and all the psychology.

Q: Reading books.

U.G.: Reading books, religious books — this is something new added on to the already existing things there, but you have not succeeded in freeing yourself from the boredom. That is the demand. You are bored with your life, with your existence, because it is very repetitive. First of all, your physical needs are very well taken care of, you see, here in this part of the world at least. So, there is no need for you to spend any more energy to survive. That part is taken care of.

When that is taken care of, the natural question that arises is very simple: "is that all that there is?" Going to the office every morning, or just being a housewife doing all the chores in the house, or sleeping, having sex, everything, you see — is that *all*? It is that demand on your part that is being exploited by these holy men. Is that all? So, those are some of the gimmicks that you are trying to fill the boredom there.

It's an empty, bottomless cup. It's not even a bottomless cup, it is a bottomless pit. You can fill that all the time with every conceivable thing that you can imagine or that others can come up with, but yet the boredom is a reality; it's a fact. Sure. Otherwise you wouldn't do anything. You are just bored. Simply bored with doing the same thing again and again and again. And you don't see any meaning in this.

Q: You're not quite conscious of that boredom . . . .

U.G.: Not quite conscious of that boredom because you are looking for something to free you from what is not there. That's all that I have been emphasizing all the time. The problem is not really the boredom. You are not conscious of the existence of boredom either on the conscious level of your thinking or on the conscious level of your existence.

The attractiveness of those things, which you use to free yourself from the non-existing boredom, has really created the boredom. And those things really cannot fill this boredom which is created by that. So it goes on and on and on and on — the newer, and newer and newer techniques and methods. Every year we have a new guru coming from India with a new gimmick, with a new technique or some new therapy, you know. All kinds of things.

Q: When we talk about consciousness . . .

U.G.: Yes, yes, I know. You seem to know something about consciousness. Will you please tell me what exactly do you mean by consciousness.

Q: I don't know. I asked you that question.

U.G.: Why are you asking me the question about consciousness? I am not throwing a counter-question at you. You are picking up that word "consciousness" somewhere, you see. You pick that up somewhere, and so they are talking of expanding consciousness.

Q: ...in the form of trying to get to know oneself better, trying to find the naturalness.

U.G.: Your naturalness is something that you don't have to know. You just have to let that function in its own way. Your wanting to know that demands some know-how, which you want from somebody. The functioning of the heart is a natural thing; the functioning of all the organs in your body is very natural. They are not for one moment asking themselves the question "How am I functioning?" The whole living organism has this tremendous intelligence which makes it function in a very natural way. You have separated what you call life from that. What you call life is living, which is in no way related to the functioning of this living organism.

So, naturally, you are asking the question "How to live?" You see, it is "how to live" that has really destroyed the natural way the whole thing is going on. That is where the culture steps in and tells you, "This is the way you should act and live. This is the one and the only thing that is good for you and good for the society." You want to change that, you see. What is it that you want to change? That is all that I am asking.

89

Q: I wish I knew.

U.G.: You will never know. So, what is it that you are trying now? Don't you see the absurdity of what you are doing? All this search is like trying to chase something that does not exist at all.

I always give my pet simile. We all take it for granted that there is such a thing as a horizon there. So, if you look at that and you say that it is a horizon, it sounds very simple to you. But you forget that the physical limitation, the limitation of your physical eye fixes that point there and it calls it "horizon". If you move in the direction of the horizon, the faster you move in the direction, even in a supersonic plane, the further it moves — farther and farther and farther away. What you are stuck with is only the limitation.

I also give the example of trying to overtake your shadow. As children we played this game of trying to over take our shadows — all the other boys running with you, everybody trying to over-take his own shadow. It never occurred to us then that it is this body that is casting this shadow there, and your wanting to overtake that shadow is an absurd game that you are playing. You can run for miles and miles and miles.

You know the story of Alice In Wonderland. The red queen has to run faster and faster and faster in order to keep still where she is. You see that's exactly what you are all doing. Running faster and faster and faster. But you are not moving anywhere.

All that you are doing to find exactly where you are is not moving at all. That gives you the feeling that you are working on something, you are doing something to achieve your goal, not knowing that what you are doing is totally unrelated to the natural functioning of this body. You are not acting in a natural way, because the ideal that has been placed before you by the culture has falsified the natural actions here. You are frightened of acting in a natural way because you have been told the way you should act.

Physical perfection is another one of the means. I am not saying anything against yoga. Please don't get me wrong. I am not saying anything against meditation — do meditation, do yoga — they are palliatives. If you want to keep your body supple, do it. A supple body is better than a stiff body. If, instead of creating tensions all the time, meditation gives you relief from your tensions, do it. But I am suggesting, that it is the meditation that is creating all the tensions. You first create the problem, and then you try to solve the problem. It's all right, but thank god you are not doing it very seriously.

That's the only hope you have. If you seriously meditate, you are in trouble. You will go crazy. Or, if you try to practice this awareness all the time — in your conscious as well as unconscious levels — you will be really in trouble. You will end up in the loony bin, singing loony tunes and merry melodies. You can learn the new songs from India, and sing and enjoy. That's all right, but don't do that [practice awareness] because it's something like trying to walk and watch every step you take. You will be in trouble, you will not be able to walk at all. So don't do that. It's a mechanical thing; the things that are there are running very smoothly and mechanically. You don't have to do a thing about it. The more you try to do about it, the more resistance you create.

The boredom is really the problem for you. The non-existing boredom has been created by the demand to free yourself from boredom. Since that [the demand] is not in any way helping you to be free from your boredom, but is making it more and more and more difficult to be free from this, you have to shop around. You have to search for all and every kind of gimmick to free yourself from that non-existing boredom. It is that which is keeping this going on forever and ever.

I am not giving you another gimmick or suggesting anything. I just want you to look at this, what you are doing to yourself. I am not trying to free you from something and take you away from that because I have some new product to sell. Not at all. I have no new products to sell, nor am I interested in selling anything. We just happen to be here, all of us, for some reason or the other — I don't know why we are here — so we might as well not even be exchanging ideas. That is meaningless. There is nothing to discuss here. The discussion has no meaning, because the object or the purpose of a discussion or a conversation is to understand something. So, that [discussion] is not the means to understand anything. Ultimately, what I am emphasizing all the time is, "Look here, there is nothing to understand." When that is understood, that there is nothing to understand, all these conversations become meaningless. So you get up and walk away once and for all. So I say, "Nice meeting you, and goodbye." That's all that I am saying all the time. "Nice meeting you, and goodbye."

Q: We just don't understand it.

U.G.: No, that's exactly what I am saying all the time, "Nice meeting you, and goodbye. God be with you and stay with god." That's the Spanish — stay with god — your god, your gurus, stay with them, you see. Don't disturb yourself unnecessarily. Live in hope and die in hope. And hope that you will be born again, if you accept the theories of reincarnation. One birth is bad enough.

Why would we want to be born again? We might as well handle this problem once and for all, now, and begin to live — what little is left for us. Don't bother about the world and the peace of the world.

If the question of how to be happy is dropped, then you begin to live, you see, not bothering about happiness at all. That doesn't exist, happiness doesn't exist at all. The more you want it, the more you search for it, the more unhappy you remain. They [the search and unhappiness] go together, you see.

Q: Don't you think that it goes against everything in religion, society and culture?

U.G.: Culture, all systems of thought . . .

Q: Structures, systems, all systems . . .

U.G.: All structures of thought, philosophical, religious, materialistic structures . . .

Q: Don't you think that's negative? And not just because I think it's negative, but people would say . . .

U.G.: Why are you saying it is negative? Listen . . . .

Q: ...because people say that.

U.G.: People can say that because it's an easy way out for them. You forget one thing. All the positive approaches that man has invented and used for centuries — they have not resulted in anything useful. They have not produced the results you have been promised. And yet you go on and on and on, hoping that somehow, through some miracle, you will be able to achieve your positive goals, or the goals which are placed before us through the positive approach. You keep doing it only because you have hope, and it is that hope that keeps you going.

Don't be caught up in this structure of thought which always suggests the positive and negative. Your goals are always positive. Since your goals have failed to give you the desired results, you have begun to look at these things and approach them in a negative way. The positive and negative approaches function only in the field of thought.

What I am suggesting is, look, your positive approach so far has not given you the desired results. And I am telling you why it has not given you the desired results. I am telling you why you are stuck where you are stuck. But immediately you turn around and say, "Your approach is negative." It is not at all negative. I am presenting the other side of the coin, or the other side of the picture, to neutralize your argument. Not to win you over to my point of view, or to stress the negative approach to the problems. Your goal being a positive goal, no matter what approach you adopt, it is a positive approach. You may call it a negative approach, but it is still a positive approach.

So, you must be very, very clear about the goal. What I am trying to emphasize is that the goal must go.

Q: You leave the goal?

U.G.: It has no meaning at all. The goal has no meaning. The goal which you have placed before yourself has no meaning at all, because it has resulted only in struggle, pain and sorrow. You

94

are using will, as I said a while ago, and the will has a certain limitation. You can't use it beyond a certain limit.

The use of your will and the use of your effort gives you a sort of additional energy to tackle these problems and to face these problems, but actually it is limited in its scope. The energy that you produce is only a frictional energy. The will creates friction, and that friction gives you some sort of energy. But that energy cannot last long, and so you are back again in square one.

Q: I think you also realize that the whole western-christian civilization is built upon the goal.

U.G.: Why just western civilization? All civilizations, all cultures place before you a goal. Whether it is a material goal or a spiritual goal. There are ways and means of achieving your material goals, but even in this respect there is a lot of pain, there is a lot of suffering. And you have superimposed on that what is called a spiritual goal.

Whereas in the material world the goal is something tangible. The instrument which you are using to achieve your material goal does produce certain results. By using that more and more you can achieve the desired results. But there is no guarantee.

The instrument which you are using is limited in its scope. It is applicable only in this [material] area.

So, the instrument which you are using to achieve your so-called spiritual goals is the same instrument. You do not realize that all the spiritual goals that are superimposed on your so-called material goals are born out of your fantasy, because you have divided life into material and spiritual. It doesn't matter what instrument you use to achieve your goal, whether it is material or spiritual, it is exactly the same.

Q: Is it not true that we, as human beings, are active. Even plants are active, living beings. We are not passive. We must have some sort of a goal. Are you saying that it is bad to have . . .

U.G.: I want you to be very clear about the goal. What do you want? What do you want? It is not the want that is wrong. But the only way you can achieve your material or spiritual goals is through the instrument which you use to achieve your material goals. What I am suggesting is, that the only instrument you have is thinking.

See, I want to be a millionaire. A millionaire wants to be a billionaire, and a billionaire wants to be a trillionaire. So, that is the goal. A happy man would never want to be happy. You want to be more and more happy. Or, you want to be permanently happy. Sure. You are happy sometimes and you are unhappy some other times. So, you want pleasures and you want those pleasures to be permanent. And at the same time, you also know that the so-called demand for pleasure, temporary or otherwise, is giving you pain as well. The goal of every person in this world, whether he is here in the west or in the east or even in communist countries — is exactly the same. So, what he wants is to have pleasure without pain at all. And to be happy always, without even a moment of unhappiness. What he is actually struggling and striving hard for, is to achieve this impossible goal of having one [happiness] without the other [unhappiness].

Q: But that isn't true of old people.

U.G.: Everybody.

Q: But older people know that there is no pleasure without pain. There is no luck without bad luck, because you cannot speak of luck if you don't know what bad luck is. Older people know that everybody gets his portion of bad luck and suffering. And those people are not thinking of getting pleasure without pain. They know they get pain.

U.G.: And yet, you see, they want to make it possible to be without pain. Sure. That's all that I am saying. Whether they are consciously doing it or not, that is what everybody is after. You know what will give you happiness.

Q: Paradise.

U.G.: If you achieve all the goals you have placed before yourself, success, money, name and fame, position or power, you are happy. In this process you are struggling hard. But you are putting a lot of will and effort into that. As long as you succeed you have no problems at all, but you cannot always succeed — you know all that.

But there is somehow hope that it will be possible for you to always succeed. You are frustrated because you find that you cannot always succeed. Yet there is still hope. Whether it is for material goals or spiritual goals, the demand is to succeed in your efforts to reach, attain or accomplish whatever goals you have placed before yourself.

You have to help me. I am not here to give any talk. So, I ask the question, repeatedly, when people come to see me — a very simple question — you must be very clear as to what you want. "I want this" or "I don't want that". It's alright. When once you know exactly what you want, you will be able to find out the ways and means of fulfilling your wants. Unfortunately, people want too many things at the same time.

So, you crystallize all of your wants into one basic want, because all the other wants are variations of the same want. You reject my suggestion that man always wants to be happy without even rare moments of unhappiness or permanent pleasure without pain, which as I said a while ago, is a physical impossibility.

The body cannot take any sensation, be it pleasurable or painful, for long. If it does, it will destroy the sensitivity of the sensory perceptions, and the sensitivity of the nervous system. The moment you recognize a particular sensation as a pleasurable sensation, naturally there is a demand to make that pleasurable sensation last longer. So, every sensation, depending upon the intensity of that sensation, which is plagued by you to invest it with more intensity or less intensity (depending upon what you are after), has a limited life of its own.

The demand comes only when you separate yourself from that pleasurable sensation and begin to think of how you can extend the limits of the pleasurable sensation or the moments of happiness. Your thinking has turned that particular demand to make this pleasurable sensation last longer than its natural duration into a problem. It has turned that into a problem for the functioning of this body, and by so doing, it has created a neurological problem. It [the body] is doing everything possible to absorb that, whereas your thinking makes it impossible for this body to handle that in its own way, for the simple reason that you are trying to solve those problems within the field of your religious or psychological approaches.

Actually, those problems are neurological problems, and if the body is left alone to handle them in its own way, it will do a better job than your trying to solve them on psychological or religious levels. All the solutions that we have been offered, and the solutions which we have been adopting for centuries, have not done any good except to give us a little bit of comfort, a palliative to help you bear the pain. Yet we are not free from that pain at all because of the hope that somehow the instrument which is turning all these things into problems can be solved through the same instrument. The only thing that this mechanism of thinking can do is to create a problem. But it can never, never, solve the problem.

If thought is not the instrument to solve the problems, is there any other instrument? I say no. It can only create the problems. It cannot solve the problems. When this understanding dawns on you, then you will realize that the energy that is there in the body, which is the manifestation of life or expression of life, handles everything in a tremendously easier way than the frictional thinking which you are generating through your ideas of how to handle these problems.

Q: So, when you feel that you have a problem you just leave it alone?

U.G.: You see when you put it that way, then there is a demand from the person who is suggesting that to ask how you can leave that alone. You know that you cannot leave it alone. You just say that you would leave it alone. Naturally the next question will be, how to leave that alone without the interference of this thought. There is no how. If anybody suggests how, you are caught up in the same vicious circle.

That is why all these therapies we have in our midst today and all those gurus we have in the market place, who are suggesting umpteen numbers of techniques, are creating this tremendous burden which does not in any way lighten the load, but on the other hand, is adding more and more burden to this situation in which you find yourself today.

All those systems and techniques cannot be of any help except that they will act as a palliative for a while so you can bear the pain for a little longer. On the other hand, they are disturbing the whole chemistry of the body, instead of being of any help for you to solve the problems for yourself.

Q: They are disturbing the chemistry?

U.G.: They are disturbing the chemistry and in this process it [the body] is throwing up all kinds of aberrations which you consider to be spiritual experiences. So, your breathing exercises, your yoga exercises, your meditations, are disturbing the chemistry of the body, and the natural rhythm of the body in exactly the same way that all these drugs which people take disturb the chemistry of the body. So, you say that they [drugs] are damaging, but actually these [spiritual techniques] are far more damaging than those things [drugs].

I am not suggesting that you should take drugs, but they serve the same purpose as all these therapies, spiritual or psychological therapies, that are being dished out day after day after day. The fact is that they give you some relief, like anacin — you have a headache and you don't even give the body an opportunity to handle it for a little while. You rush to the market and buy anacin or aspirin or something and you drug yourself. In exactly the same way, it makes it difficult for the body to manufacture the natural things that are there in your body to help relieve you of the pain.

The body has all the hallucinogens you are talking about as part of its system. It wants to control the pain and to relieve itself of the pain. It knows only the physical pain, and it is not interested in your psychological pain at all. The solutions they are offering are only in the area of the psychological field, but not in the physical field.

If you take aspirin, for example, it destroys the capacity of this body to handle that pain in a natural way. I am not suggesting that you should take the natural way and switch over to macrobiotics or any other funny health food stuff. That is as vicious and mischievous as any other medicine.

Q: What then is your clear advice if you have problems?

U..G.: You cannot but create the problems. You are creating the problems, number one. But actually you are not looking at the problems at all. You are not dealing with the problems. You are more interested in solutions than the problems. That makes it difficult for you to look at the problem.

I am suggesting that "Look here, you don't have any problems." You assert with all the emphasis at your command, with tremendous animation, "Look, I have a problem here."

All right, you have a problem. That problem you are talking about is something which you can pinpoint and say, "This is the problem." Physical pain is a reality. So, you go to a doctor, whether it [the medicine] is good for the body or not, whether it is a poison or not, it produces the required relief, however short it may be. But the therapies that those people are dishing out are intensifying the problem which is non-existing. You are only searching for the solutions. If there is anything to those solutions that they are offering, the problems should go, should disappear. Actually the problem is still there, but you never question the solutions that those people are offering you as a relief or as something that can free you from the problems.

If you question the solutions that have been offered to us by all those people who are marketing these goodies in the name of holiness, enlightenment, transformation, you will find they are really not the solutions. If they were the solutions, they should produce the results and free you from the problem. They do not.

You don't question the solutions because the sentiment creeps in there. "That fellow who is selling this in the marketplace cannot be a fraud, cannot be a fake." You take him to be an enlightened man or a god walking on the face the earth. That god may be fooling and killing himself, may be indulging in self-deception all the time and then selling that stuff, that shoddy piece of goods, to you. You don't question the solutions because then you will be questioning the man who is selling this. [You think] he cannot be dishonest, a holy man cannot be dishonest.

Yet you have to question the solutions because those solutions are not solving your problems. Why don't you question those solutions and put them to the test — test the validity of those solutions? When you realize that they don't work, you have to throw them out, down the drain, out of the window. But you don't do it because of the hope that somehow those solutions will give you the relief that you are after. The instrument [thought] which you are using is what has created this problem. So that instrument will never, never accept the possibility that those solutions are fake solutions. They are not the solutions at all.

The hope keeps you going. That makes it difficult for you to look at the problems. If one solution fails, you go somewhere else and pick up another solution. If that solution fails you go find another. You are shopping around for all these solutions but never once will you ask yourself, "What is the problem?"

I don't see any problem. I see only that you are interested in solutions and that you come here and ask the same question. "I want another solution." Those solutions have not helped you at all, so why do you want another solution? You will add one more to your list of solutions, but you will end up in exactly the same situation. If you find the uselessness of one, if you see one of them, you have seen them all. You don't have to try one after the other.

What I am suggesting is if that is the solution you should be free from the problem. If that is not the solution, then there is nothing that you can do about it; and then the problem is not even there. So, you are not interested in solving the problem, because that will put an end to you. You want the problems to remain. You want the hunger to remain because if you are not hungry you will not seek this food from all these holy men. What they are giving you are some scraps, bits of food, and you are satisfied. Even assuming for a moment that he [the spiritual leader or therapist] can give you the whole loaf of bread, which he cannot do, he will only promise to keep it here, hidden somewhere. Promises — bit by bit, bit by bit — he gives you. And thereby you are not dealing with the problem of hunger, but you are more interested in getting a bit more from that fellow who is promising you a solution rather than dealing with your problem of hunger. You are not dealing with the problem of hunger, but you are more interested in getting more crumbs from that fellow, than dealing with your problem of hunger.

Q: It's like going to a movie, running away from reality.

U.G.: You never look at the problem. What is the problem with anger, for example. I don't want to discuss all those silly things which these people have been discussing for centuries. Anger. Where is that anger? Can you separate the anger from the functioning of this body? It's like a wave in the ocean. Can you separate the waves from the ocean. You can sit there and wait until the waves subside, so that you can have a swim in the ocean (like King Canute who sat there for years and years hoping that the waves in the ocean would disappear so that he could have a swim in a calm ocean). That will never happen. You can sit there and learn all about the waves, the high tide and the low tide (the scientists have given us all kinds of explanations), but the knowledge about that is not going to be of any help to you.

You are not really dealing with anger at all. Where do you feel the anger, first of all? Where do you feel all these so-called problems you want to be free from? . . . the desires? The burning desires. The desire burns you. Hunger burns you. So, the solutions you have or the means of fulfilling them [desire and hunger] are

104

very simple and make it impossible for that to burn itself out in your system.

Where do you feel the fear? You feel it here in the pit of your stomach. It is part of the body. The body cannot take those high and low tides of energy, so you want to suppress it for some spiritual or social reasons. You are not going to succeed.

Anger is energy, a tremendous outburst of energy. And by destroying that energy through any means, you are destroying the very expression of life itself. It becomes a problem only when you try to do something with that energy. When it is absorbed by the system, you will not do the things that you think you will do if the anger is left alone. You are actually not dealing with the anger, but the frustration. Or to avoid such a situation which has resulted in clumsiness in your relationships or in your understanding of yourself. You want to be prepared to meet such situations as and when they arise in the future.

The instrument which you are using has been used by you every time there is an outburst of anger. Yet you have not succeeded in freeing yourself from the anger. You won't come into the position of anything extraordinary, other than this instrument which you have been using all these years, and at the same time you hope that somehow this very thing will help you to be free from anger tomorrow. It is the same hope.

Q: But if somebody is very angry, he or she may become violent.

U.G.: That violence is absorbed by the body.

Q: And threatening.

U.G.: To whom?

Q: To other people.

U.G.: Yes. So? So what?

Q: Running around with a knife . . . .

U.G.: So what?

Q: Killing somebody.

U.G.: Yes. Why are *you* killing people, thousands of people, for no fault of theirs. Why you are limiting something which is natural, but you are not condemning the nations that are dropping bombs on helpless people? Do you call them sane? Both of them have sprung from the same source. As long as you do anything to control your anger here, you will indulge in such atrocious things and justify them, because that is the only way to protect your way of life and your way of thinking. These two things go together. Why do you justify that? That is insane.

He is not hurting you, but he is threatening your way of life. There is a danger of that man taking away what you consider to be your precious things. This idea of stopping this man from acting when there is an outburst of anger is exactly the same. The religious man has found that an angry man will be an anti-social man.

As long as he practices virtues, so long he will remain an anti-social man, and he will act out of anger. When the goal that the society has placed before you, when that same goal which you adopted for yourself as an ideal goal to be practiced, is finished for you, you will not harm *anybody*, either individually or collectively as a nation.

You have to deal with the anger. But you are dealing with something totally unrelated to the anger, not even once do you let that anger burn itself out within the framework where it originates and functions. Having some therapy of hitting your pillows, hitting this, that, and the other, is just a joke. That does not free the man from the anger once and for all.

Q: Hitting on a pillow?

U.G.: That's what they do, one of the therapies they have.

Q: It doesn't help?

U.G.: It [the anger] will appear again. So what do you do? You are not dealing with anger. You will never deal with this anger at all as long as you are interested in finding out a way of not hitting the person who is coming at you with a knife. You have to protect yourself, that is essential. I am not saying for a moment that your anger makes it impossible for you to deal with that situation. Don't say that it's non-violence or you should not hurt somebody else. You never practice that. Of course, they practice it on a larger scale, but in daily life they say it is something terrible to do. I don't see any problem with that at all. What is the problem?

There is no point in discussing those hypothetical situations for the simple reason that the person who is hopping mad with anger, burning with anger, will not seek to discuss the question of anger. That is amazing. That's the time to deal with those things, when you are really burning with anger, burning with desire, burning with all those things that you want to be free from. Otherwise, it becomes a classroom discussion. Somebody talking on the anatomy of anger, the anatomy of how the anger arises, or the anatomy of love. It's too ridiculous. They offer solutions which don't work when there is a real situation. That's the reason why I don't discuss all these things. No problem. There's no problem for the individual. When he's mad with anger — that's the time for him to deal with it. It stops the thinking.

Q: U.G., is there a possibility of looking at the problem?

U.G.: No. Because you are yourself the problem.

Q: So, there is no answer?

U.G.: There is no way of separating yourself from the problem. That's what you are trying to do. That is what I mean by saying that you are putting anger out there and trying to look at and deal with it as if it is an object outside of you. When you separate yourself, the only result is exactly what you fear would happen. That is inevitable. So you have no way of controlling that at all. Is there anything that you can do to prevent this separation from what you are? It is a horrible thing to realize that you are yourself anger and whatever you do to stop that, prevent it, or do something about it, is false. That [preventing, etc.] will be tomorrow or in your next life — not now. So that is what you are.

You are not a spiritual man or a religious man. You can imagine that you are a religious man, because you are trying to control your anger, or trying to be free from anger, or trying to be less and less angry as the years go by. All that makes you feel that you are not that vicious man whom you avoid. You are no different. You are not any more spiritual than the people whom you condemn.

Tomorrow you are going to be a marvelous person, you will be free from anger. What do you want me to do in the meantime? Admire you? Because you have put on the label that you are a spiritual man or that you have put on fancy robes? What do you want me to do? For that you want me to admire you? There is nothing there to be admired because you are as vicious as anybody else in this world. Condemning that has no meaning. Adopting a posture which is totally unrelated to what is happening there has no meaning either.

So, how can you put on this posture or adopt some kind of an attitude and feel superior to the animals. The animals are better than the humans. If there is a threat, the animal acts and that is only for the purpose of survival. If you kill your fellow man to feed yourself that is a moral act — only for that purpose, because if you look around, one form of life lives on another form of life. And if you talk of vegetarianism and kill millions of people, that is the most immoral, unpardonable act that a civilized culture of human beings can ever do. Do you see the absurdity of the two? You condemn this [killing]. You love the animals. What for?

What about the human beings you are murdering and massacring simply because they are a threat to you? They are one day going to take away everything you have. So, in anticipation of those people coming and robbing everything, you think you have a right to massacre them in the name of your beliefs, in the name of god knows what. That is what religions have done right from the beginning. So, what is the point in reviving all those religions? What is the point in all those hosts of gurus coming into these countries preaching something that does not operate in their own lives or in the countries they come from. They can talk of oneness of life, and unity of life, all the time. But it doesn't operate in their own lives. What does it mean? You condemn this simple thing that is necessary for your survival. That's a very moral action. Not to survive, not to feed yourself is an act of perversion.

So you suffer in the hope of getting a permanent seat there in heaven — non-existing heaven. You are going through hell now in the hope of reaching heaven after your death. What for ? So suffer.

All religions emphasize that. Bear the pain, the endurance of pain is the means. You go through hell in the hope of having paradise at the end of your life, or the end of a series of lives if you want to believe that. I am just pointing out the absurdity of talking about these things. The religious [teaching] has no meaning when you are pushed into a corner. Then you will behave exactly like anybody else. So this culture, your values, religious or otherwise, haven't touched a bit there.

If man is freed from this moral dilemma, which has been the basis of the whole thinking of man, then he will live like a human being. Not a spiritual man, not a religious man. A religious man is no good for the society. A kind man is a menace to the society (one who is practicing kindness as a fine art).

Q: ... is a menace?

U.G.: He is a menace of the society because all the destruction has come from them [religious teachers]. One who talks of love, one who talks of "love thy neighbor as thyself", one who talks about non-violence — all the destructive forces originated in the thinking of that man. So, we are all the inheritors of that culture. We cannot do anything but that. [If you reject those teachers] you are freed from the burden and the falseness of the whole culture. That's all that I am saying. Individually you are freed from the totality of all the absurdities that have been imposed upon us. That's all that I am saying.

Q: I can't accept that there are not some (for instance Jesus, not Christianity, not the church), who are real people.

U.G.: You can't accept it. I know. Why did they put him on the cross and nail him to death?

Q: They made a god out of man. I don't agree with that.

U.G.: Not even an ordinary man, because he made statements out of which the whole dogmatic teaching of Christianity originated. Certainly.

That applies to every teacher. All the teachers whom we consider to be the great religious teachers of mankind, let alone those people who are doing holy business in the market place today. We are not concerned about this. There is no use blaming them anyway.

So, we are here. We are the inheritors of all that violent culture. Your culture is nothing but to teach man how to kill and how to be killed, whether it is in the name of religion, or in the name of political ideology, or in the name of patriotism, or anything you want. It can't be any different. That is why I say that the whole thing is moving in the direction of the total annihilation of man.

Such things have set in motion forces of destruction which no power can stop.

Q: Yes. No power.

U.G.: No power, no god can stop it because those gods themselves have set in motion these forces of destruction. You see that now happening. When the caveman used the jawbone of an ass to kill his neighbor, there were chances of survival for others. The same caveman today who lives there in the Kremlin and in the White house, and in the Parliament House there in India — they are the ones who will set in motion, who will let loose forces of destruction that will completely wipe out every form of life on this planet. And man will take with him every species that exists today on this planet.

It has all come out of that thinking of the man who taught religion to men, who wanted to establish love on the face of this earth. And see what he has made out of it!

Q: So, if you say we can't stop it . . . .

U.G.: Can you? Can you stop it? You can't stop it. So the one thing that you can do is to . . . .

Q: I think that as humanity we can stop it if we want to.

U.G.: When? Well, you don't want to obviously. Do you want to?

Q: Yes.

U.G.: Then how do you go about it? How do you go about it, tell me. Do you see the urgency of the whole situation? Some lunatic there may press the button. We sit here comfortably and talk about these things . . . .

Q: I think there is a possibility we can stop it.

U.G.: What is the possibility?

Q: To act.

U.G.: How? When are you going to act? When the tide is too late. When the whole thing, the holocaust, is released it will be too late. Or, you can join the anti-bomb movement — which is ridiculous.

Q: It's ridiculous?

U.G.: Yes, of course.

Q: It's too late?

U.G.: Don't you want the police to protect your tiny little property? The hydrogen bomb is an extension of the same. You can't say this [the police] I want, and that [the bomb] I don't want. It is an extension of the same.

Q: So, we are helpless?

U.G.: What makes you think that it is possible for you to stop this? You can stop it in you. Free yourself from that social structure that is operating in you without becoming anti-social, without becoming a reformer, without becoming anti-this, anti-that. You can throw the whole thing out of your system and free yourself from the burden of this culture, for yourself and by yourself. Whether it has any usefulness for society or not is not your concern. If there is one individual who walks free, you won't have any more the choking feeling of what this horrible culture has done to you. It's neither east nor west, it's all the same. Human nature is exactly the same — there's no difference.

You are only interested in what to do, what to do.

Q: We all are.

U.G.: How can we stop? Individually there isn't a damn thing that you can do. Collectively you can create a salvation army or something like that. That's all. So what?

Q: What do I think about such an answer? I do agree, but it's very theoretical. Just free yourself of the burden of culture. I understand it. But practically it's very difficult, of course. There's nothing I can do about it.

U.G.: There's nothing, not a thing.... You have no freedom of action at all.

Q: No.

U.G.: When that is understood, what is there expresses itself. The intelligence that is there can function much more effectively than all the solutions that man has come up with through his thinking, which is the result of millions, and millions and millions of years of evolution. The ideal that we have placed before us, the perfect man, is just a myth. Such a man doesn't exist at all. The ideal man doesn't exist. It is just a word, an idea. All your life you are trying to become that ideal man and what you are left with is the misery, the suffering, the hope to be that. "One day, you will see." That's the hope. We will die with that hope.

Q: So, one solution is to accept your being here, as you are.

U.G.: As you are, exactly the way you are. Then you are not in conflict with society. Culture has put the demand in you that is pushing you in the direction of wanting to change yourself into something. That is what the culture has done, put it in you. If you want to do something, they say, "Boy, look here, watch your step." That is what they are doing. The second movement that comes, that is the society. "Watch your step" it says. So, that has put fear in you. Then, at the same time, it talks of freeing yourself from fear, and having courage and the whole thing — "be a peerless man" — that is only for the purpose of using you as a pawn in maintaining the status quo of society.

That is why it is teaching courage, it is teaching fearlessness, so that it can use you to maintain the continuity of the society. You are a part of that. That is why every time you want to act, what is there is fear and the impossibility of acting. The society is not out there, the culture is not out there, and unless you are free from that you cannot act.

Q: Unless, you are free from it.

U.G.: Then you will not come here and ask me the question "What will be that action?" There is an action already. There is an action as far as you are concerned.

Q: So, do you mean that man is only entitled to act when he is free from society? Are you free?

U.G.: Man is not able to act, because he is all the time thinking in terms of the freedom to act. "How can I be free to act?" That's all that you are concerned about, the freedom. But you are not acting that freedom. The demand for the freedom to act is preventing the action, which is neither social nor anti-social.

Q: So, you are free if you accept yourself and your situation?

U.G.: That's all, you are not in conflict with the society any more. That's the reality of the world. Whether you will be of any use to the society or not. Actually, you will not be any use to the society. On the other hand, if you become a threat to the society, the society will liquidate you. Because you are disturbing all the movements in the direction of status quo.

You are a neurotic because you want two things at the same time. It is that which has created this problem for you — wanting two things at the same time. [First] You want to bring about a change in yourself. Change is the demand of society, so that you can become a part of that, and maintain the continuity of the social structure. The second thing is, you don't want to change. This is the conflict.

When the demand for bringing up any change in you ceases, then the concern to change the world around you also comes to an end, *ipso facto*. Both of them are finished. Otherwise, your actions will be a danger to the society. They will liquidate you, that's for sure. So, you are ready to be liquidated by that social structure, that is the courage. Not to die in the battlefields, and to fight for your flag.

What does a flag symbolize? You wave your flag here, they wave their flag, and then both of them talk of peace. How absurd the whole situation is. And yet you talk about peace. You owe allegiance to your flag and they owe allegiance to their flag, and you are at the same time talking of peace in this world? How can there be any peace in this world when you are waving your flag here, and they are waving their flag? Whoever has better weapons will have the day for himself. With my flag here, your flag there — these peace marches — or you create another flag with the anti-bomb groups.

Q: It's useless.

U.G.: I don't have to tell you. Are you ready to do away with the policeman? Individually you want to protect yourself, your life, or your little property. I am not saying whether you should or should not. You need the help of the policeman to protect it. So, you draw a line and say "This is my nation." You want to protect your nation. And, when you cannot do it, you will have to expand your means of destruction also to protect yourself, and you will say it is for defensive purposes. Certainly it is defensive. That [the bomb] is only an extension of this [the policeman]. You can't talk against that as long as you want this policeman to protect your things. You can sit around there, go on peace marches, sit around those nuclear reactors and sing peace songs and play guitars, and "make love not war" — don't listen to all that crap. Making love and making war spring from the same source. It becomes a sham mockery.

That's enough I think. That's enough.

Q: So what is this relation between ourselves and the world we live in?

U.G.: Absolutely nothing except that the world you experience is the one that is created by you. You are living in a world of your own. You have created a world of your own experiences and you are trying to project it onto the world. You have no way of experiencing the reality of the world at all. You and I use the same word to describe a video camera. What you are holding is a pen, or a pencil, as the case may be. So, we have to accept all these things as valid because they are workable. They help us to function in this world, to communicate only on that level intelligently.

Q: So, nobody can be an example for anybody else?

U.G.: Following is only for the animals, not for humans. A human being cannot follow anybody. Physically you have to depend on others, but that is all there is to it.

Q: Would you say that there is no such thing as growth in spirituality? Or could you say that . . . .

U.G.: What I am suggesting is that there is no such thing as spirituality at all. If you superimpose what you call spirituality on what is called material life, then you create problems for yourself.

Because you see growth, and development in the material world around you, you are applying that same principle to this so-called spiritual life also.

Q: Do you suggest that the problem starts when you start separating things?

U.G.: Separating things, dividing things into material life, and spiritual life. There is only one life. This is a material life, and that other has no relevance. Wanting to change your material life into that so-called religious pattern given to you, placed before you by these religious people, is destroying the possibility of your living in harmony and accepting the reality of this material world exactly the way it is. That is responsible for your pain, for your suffering, for your sorrow.

It is a constant struggle on your part to be like that and to chase something that does not exist. And that has no meaning at all. That gives you the feeling that doing is all that is important for you. Not the actual achievement of that. You are moving farther and farther away [from your goal]. The more effort you put into it, the more you feel good. Like the problems you have. Trying to solve the problems is all that is important to you, but the solutions are more interesting to you than the problems. You are more interested in solutions than looking at the problem. What is the problem, I say. You have no problems, only solutions. What is the problem? Nobody tells me what the problem is.

You are telling me that these are all the solutions. "Which one should I use to solve my problem?" What exactly is the problem? The material problems are understandable. If you don't have health, you have to do something about your health. If you don't have money, you have to do something about money. These are understandable. If you have some psychological problems, then the real problem begins. All these psychologists and the religious people with their therapies and their solutions are trying to help you, but they don't lead you anywhere, do they? The individual remains as shallow and as empty as before. What do they want to prove to themselves?

Q: You believe that problems solve themselves by going along with your own life?

U.G.: What is the problem? You never look at the problem. It is not possible for you to look at the problem as long as you are interested in the solutions.

Q: Don't you want solutions?

U.G.: You are only interested in solutions, not in solving the problem.

Q: Isn't that the same thing then?

U.G.: In that process, you find out that those solutions are really worthless. Those solutions don't solve your problem, whatever is the problem. Those solutions keep the problems going. They don't solve them. If there is something wrong with your tape recorder, or the television, that can be remedied — there is a technician who can help you. But this is an endless process going on and on and on and on, all your life. More and more of something and less and less of the other.

You never question the solutions. If you really question the solutions you will have to question the ones who have offered you those solutions. But sentimentality stands in the way of your rejecting not only the solutions, but those who have offered you the solutions. Questioning that requires a tremendous courage on your part. You can have the courage to climb the mountain, swim the lakes, go on a raft to the other side of the Atlantic or Pacific. That any fool can do, but the courage to be on your own, to stand on your two solid feet, is something which cannot be given by somebody. You cannot free yourself of that burden by trying to develop that courage. If you are freed from the burden of the entire past of mankind, then what is left there is the courage.

AFTERWORD

◄─────►

Ellen Chrystal

When U.G. was having these conversations in Amsterdam, I was living in the "spiritual community" of Da Free John. It was three years later, in 1985, that I left that community. I found myself, after 10 years of "practice," out on my ass, no money, no home, no relationship to family or old friends — and with a lot of unfinished business of my own, such as three children whom I had left in order to go "realize enlightenment".

Although I tried in many ways to fill the spiritual void that my years of participation with Da Free John had filled, I was beginning to sense that all of my attempts to find religious and spiritual meaning in life were somehow false — an imposition on the very simple fact of nature itself. Yet seeking had become such a habit, I could not stop.

In 1987 I was on a three day retreat with Bernadette Roberts (an ex-Carmelite nun, who has realized a state she calls "no self"). As the retreat was nearing its end, an old friend of mine (another Da Free John divorcee, as U.G. calls us) handed a book to Bernadette called "The Mystique of Enlightenment." It was by U.G. Krishnamurti. Bernadette handed it back to my friend, and I quickly said, "If you don't mind, I would like to read that."

With book in hand, I withdrew to my cabin. The first thing I noticed was U.G.'s droll disclaimer at the beginning of the book:

"This book has no copyright . . ." (this was quite exhilarating after having spent the past ten years with a man who claimed a perpetual copyright on every word he uttered).

During the last few hours of the retreat I read the book from cover to cover. I was reading what I felt in my gut was the direct and simple expression of a truth I had been searching for all my life. Yet I was completely unable to do a thing about it. Actually, for that matter, it was the beginning of the end of doing anything about enlightenment at all.

Eventually, I wrote to the publisher in India, inquiring about U.G.'s whereabouts and whether I could meet him. After many weeks, I received a letter from a man named Chandrashekar. U.G. was travelling. I could contact Julie Thayer, who just happened to live a few blocks from me on the Upper West Side of New York City.

I called Julie. She invited me over to her apartment, and within minutes I was at her doorstep. Julie had just completed an around-the-world trip with U.G. and had taken video footage of him everywhere they went. There were about 100 hours of unedited tapes. For several weeks I went to Julie's apartment every day and sat mesmerized, watching this odd man as he wandered around the world, meeting and conversing with an eclectic assortment of people. Soon after that, U.G. came to the United States and I flew to San Rafael, California to meet him for the first time.

"Why have you wasted your money?" he asked me when we first met. "I wanted to meet you," I answered. "You won't get anything here," he told me, adding, "if you got anything at all from my books you wouldn't be here." What could I say. Something was going on, but it was certainly nothing I could explain or make use of. I had no frame of reference for this guy. All my guru-worship lessons from the past were of no use here. But, at the same time, he was clearly no ordinary man.

All one can do when they first meet U.G is observe how he

functions. After years of bowing and scraping at the feet of Da Free John, it was quite refreshing to sit around with someone, who seemed to me to be in a state I would call "enlightened" (don't tell U.G. I said that), and not have to perform any ceremony or make any effort to express anything in particular. I could just be myself, whatever that was.

U.G. moves like a cat. Economy of motion. He also grows on one. Some people are not interested in what he has to say, and that's fine with him, because he really does not believe he has any message at all. Others hang on every word, and those he constantly confronts and confounds. Others (I guess I fall into this category), listen, and then just live their lives. I believe he has saved me from years of futile seeking, and he has also lightened my conceptual load in a very real sense. He has become part of my life without intruding in any way. It is very interesting to me, and extremely difficult (as others will attest) to communicate.

I now have had the opportunity to spend time with U.G. in New York City, California and Gstaad, Switzerland. Each time and place was quite different, and yet very much the same. I could tell all kinds of interesting anecdotes, but then U.G. doesn't like "testimonials".

I had the "Give Up" series of audio-cassettes for a few years before I actually listened to them. When I did listen, I was very drawn to these conversations. They seemed to be a composite of U.G.'s most fundamental expression. Of course, reading these edited conversations is not quite the same as listening to the voice which expresses these bombshells, but the written word has its own effect.

U.G. does not give lectures. He does not write books. Every word written about him has been produced by friends who are simply moved to do so. Like a master jazzman, he is given the key, the tempo, the chord changes by whomever he is with, and then he merely responds.

In these Amsterdam conversations, U.G. creates a structure that makes sense — and even if you can't quite hold on to it, you can come back again and again, and each time hear some new "rif" that you may have missed before. And it sets you straight just a bit more. It lightens your load just a bit more.

Thanks, U.G.

Ellen J. Chrystal
November 1995